Design Lives Here

For Chris

Design Lives Here

Australian interiors, furniture and lighting

Penny Craswell

Contents

Introduction

Gestalt psychology is a theory of perception that says that the particular cannot be understood except in relation to the whole; a part's significance only emerges in the context of its surroundings. In contrast, design writing tends to focus on an object's design and making. The object itself is simply a product to be sold. But, of course, the story of the object in context is just as important as its origins as a design concept and a made form. You don't perceive a chair in a void, without any connection to the real world. You experience it in a room, in real time, as you use it.

Theories of narrative in object design explore how stories are attached to objects, and these stories are not necessarily connected to the object's design. In fact, as Dagmar Steffen, design theorist at the Lucerne School of Art and Design, says, 'The design of the object often has no or rather little influence on its status as a beloved object'.

The interior design of a home is constructed from these object stories, especially for 'ethos-intensive objects', which US design theorists Dana Vaux and David Wang describe as providing 'points of shared understanding between the designer and the culture of the client'. Interior designers must understand not only what kind of house or apartment their client needs, and design for their lifestyle and behaviours, but also the beliefs, attitudes and values their client holds, and create a space filled with objects that carry a certain meaning. Designers must also consider how meaning will be attached to these objects in the future.

< The view from the dining room to the kitchen at Apartment 1906 in Sydney, designed by Amber Road.

Design Lives Here features beautiful homes designed by some of Australia's leading architects and interior designers. Within each home, I have highlighted one piece of Australian-designed furniture or lighting. The objects are key pieces, integral to the design of the home and how each space is experienced.

The spaces and objects are connected by the design process. In each case, the architect/interior designer and furniture/lighting designer has sketched their design, weighed up functional and aesthetic concerns, and selected the materials and processes that are best suited to creating a beautiful, long-lasting design. Both space and object are also connected by their user and experienced over time – ordinary days, one after the other, where you sit in this chair, in this room.

In this book, I tell stories of the origins of design – of both home and object. For the owners of Allen Key House, the purchase of the HB table as the key design piece for their living and dining space was a journey of discovery about Australian design itself, via Koskela's showroom. Learning about this brand and its furniture led directly to their decision to purchase the table.

In Perth's House A by Whispering Smith, the Donny stool by local designer Guy Eddington was one of a number of different design features brought to the project by makers in the area. Architect Kate Fitzgerald also brought in a carpenter and a steelworker and even had the concrete panels of the building cast on site. At Smart Design Studio's project, Indigo Slam, the entire contents of the house was a huge creative project for Adelaide furniture designer Khai Liew, whose team of joiners and artisans constructed 109 key pieces of furniture, rugs and other items designed specifically for this project.

At Treetop House, with interiors by Arent&Pyke, the apartment is filled with incredible furniture, lighting and artworks. Each decision was made in the context of the design team's acute sensibilities of the design world at large, in combination with their consideration of the client's needs. And at Noble Hughes House, the owners were already huge fans of mid-century fashion and collectables when they began this project. As a result, they bought a number of vintage Grant Featherston chairs from the 1950s, including the glorious Wing Contour armchair.

How each object relates to the interior of its home is discussed in more detail in the chapters ahead, but what of the houses and apartments themselves? If each object exists within the context of its home, then each of the twenty-one homes featured in this book also has its own context. Many of the designers have taken inspiration from the land, the site or the surrounding city. Others have responded to Australia's relaxed lifestyle and its unique natural beauty, history and culture.

The different homes in *Design Lives Here* provide clues about the character of Australian residential design. While this book does include expansive, beautiful houses in rural locations, the truth is that Australia is one of the most urbanised (or suburbanised) countries on earth. This is reflected in the projects in this book, which are, more often than not, updated versions of existing building types familiar to most Australians – the terrace house, the Californian bungalow, the Queenslander. But that doesn't mean that Australian residential homes aren't changing. Our houses and apartments are influenced by new social factors: smaller dwellings on less land, urban infill, shared and intergenerational living, short-stay rentals and an ageing population. Millennial architects, interior designers and owners are rethinking the old ways. The Australian dream of owning a quarter-acre block with a picket fence and a garage is no longer relevant – or at least no longer so simple.

Design Lives Here includes houses and apartments – large and small – designed for families, couples and singles, with budgets that range from high-end to modest. There are dreamy harbour views in the city (Doorzien House by Bijl Architecture), rural locations with panoramic ocean views (The Headland by Atelier Andy Carson), city apartments with an urban edge (Fitzroy Loft by Architects EAT) and interesting approaches to the suburban setting (Kiah House by Austin Maynard Architects).

There are playful houses (Untitled 06 by Bagnoli Architects), large houses for entertaining (Kew Residence by Doherty Design Studio), houses whose stories revolve around a single material (Armadale House by B.E Architecture) and houses steeped in history (Port Officer's House by Birrelli). Diversity of place, scale and style abounds.

What these homes share is a contemporary sensibility – there are no faux historical styles here – and a sensitivity to site; bespoke architecture and interior design mean these houses and apartments are designed for their owners and for their cities, towns and suburbs.

In Australia, our history and isolation from the rest of the world have influenced our design approach. We are free from many of the trappings of history faced in Europe, where crumbling ruins must be negotiated on every street corner. Instead, we are free to make our own style – and to create our own stories of our homes and the objects that reside in them.

Brick House

+ Glissando credenza

ARCHITECT

Andrew Burges Architects

—

DESIGNER

Jon Goulder

Shifting topographies

Clad inside and out in a slender, pale brick, this house is remarkable for bringing the exteriors inside in a series of layered spaces. Subtle shifts in level create a sense of topography, while bridges connect second-storey rooms across gaping voids. Architect Andrew Burges describes it as creating a microgeography within the macrogeography that is Bondi – and Sydney. 'Through my architecture practice, I've tried to shape projects around how architecture contributes to the geography of the place – that sense that you can be an agent of positive change, working into and accentuating the geographical conditions of Sydney.'

Walking into this house in a quiet street around the corner from Bondi Beach, you immediately get a sense of how space has been manipulated. A change of level up a few stairs takes you left to a small living room with a low ceiling, or ahead, past the pantry and into a grand double-height void. This sense of shifting topography continues throughout the house, helping to create a sense of intimacy despite its large size; this is a two-storey house with five bedrooms, a study and associated living rooms.

The lower storey is clad in a distinctive, elegant brick that was requested by the client, sourced in Europe and originally designed by famous architect Peter Zumthor for the Kolumba Museum in Cologne, Germany. Above, the bedrooms and other private spaces are divided into three sections by two double-height voids, with rooms across the void linked by footbridges. This

∧ The ceiling height changes from the dining space to the kitchen.

‹ Large windows and a double-height void flood the space with light.

∧ External materials, such as brick and blackened timber, are brought inside.

› The 6-millimetre wrap around the kitchen joinery is both stylish and hard-wearing.

offers a separation between the central zone, for guests and the play area, the front zone for kids' bedrooms, and the back zone for the parents' bedroom, ensuite and study. The separation adds to the sense of intimacy, breaking up this large house into a series of smaller, more friendly zones.

The voids are magnificent, mainly thanks to two huge windows with no visible evidence of window framing on either side of the second storey. Viewed from the footbridges and living spaces below, they create a sense of seamless sky. This, in combination with the outdoor materials used to clad the void spaces, makes you feel as if you are outdoors. Blackened timber wall panelling wraps the upper walls inside and corresponding first-floor walls outside. This contrasts with the private spaces, like the living rooms and bedrooms, where more domestic materials have been used. In this way, the internal envelope has been wrapped with external materials to create its own geography.

The windows from the bedrooms and bathrooms that look onto the void have shutters without glass that open out, allowing views through to other rooms and voids, and a glimpse of sky. This house is designed for a family with three young boys, and you can imagine the fun of playing, spying and other high jinks these crossings and openings offer. They are like a series of small buildings set within the larger house, creating a little community.

"I've tried to shape projects around how architecture contributes to the geography of the place – that sense that you can be an agent of positive change, working into and accentuating the geographical conditions of Sydney."

— Andrew Burges

Robust materials were required for boisterous family living, so Burges made sure that the materials were hard-wearing – a 6-millimetre wrap around the kitchen joinery doors and drawers ensures a long life and gives a furniture feel. The other star of the space is Australian design. The owner's passion for local designers and creators is reflected in the choice of pendant lights by emerging Melbourne design studio Coco Flip, and custom timber dining table and Glissando credenza designed by Adelaide furniture designer Jon Goulder.

This helps the building feel truly Australian – an Aussie-designed house with Aussie-designed furniture and lighting pieces. Burges is divided when it comes to whether national identity is important in Australian architecture or if we're all global now. He sees himself as working within the parameters of the city and the site. 'Sydney has a series of attributes – some good, some bad – that I always feel I'm working within.' It wasn't until he returned from living in the US that he realised how unique we are. 'I was speaking on the phone to someone in the US and they said, "What is that noise?" It was just the birds in the morning.'

∧ An outdoor space runs along the side to the back of the house.

⌐ The entryway features a timber shelf and peg-board for keys and bags, while concrete stairs lead to a raised living space.

< The sunken living room opens onto the exterior deck.

∧ The upstairs living zones are connected by walkways and multiple openings.

› Joinery in the bedrooms is in a light timber, creating a contrast to the black-stained cladding used to define the void spaces.

» The two-storey void features a footbridge, a large skylight and several openings.

The windows from the bedrooms and bathrooms that look onto the void have shutters without glass that open out, allowing views through to other rooms ...

⟨ Materials from the rest of the house continue into the bathroom.

《 Shutters open into the double-height void, linking the bedrooms to the living area below.

BRICK HOUSE

LOCATION
Bondi, New South Wales

——

DETAILS
Two-storey house; 5 bedrooms, 4 bathrooms; 310 m²

——

ARCHITECT
Andrew Burges Architects

——

BUILDER
Kraken Projects Pty Ltd

——

PHOTOGRAPHY
Peter Bennetts

GLISSANDO CREDENZA

DESIGNER
Jon Goulder

————

MATERIALS
Solid walnut, powder-coated steel legs

————

DETAILS OF CONSTRUCTION/MAKING
Hand-carved walnut facade on walnut carcass; powder-coated steel legs

————

PHOTOGRAPHY
Bo Wong

Carved from a single block

A furniture designer and maker by trade, Jon Goulder thought his days of making the Glissando credenza were behind him when he left Perth to become the creative director of furniture at the Jam Factory in Adelaide. 'I swore I'd never make another one when I left Perth,' he says. He threw out all of the jigs and patterns, thinking he was moving on and wouldn't produce the credenza again. But it was not to be. Goulder picked up the tools again specifically to hand carve the Glissando for the Brick House in Bondi. 'It's a crazy process,' he says. 'I carved the doors by hand from a single block to create the pattern.'

Going through it all again made Goulder realise just how much people love this original, Australian-designed and Australian-made credenza. And it's had so much interest that, since then, he has had all the tools remade. 'That project was driven by the client's passion for my work and I love my work to go to a house like that.' The joy of remaking the work fuelled his love of the design and he thought it should be in the marketplace again.

Goulder makes everything himself at the bench, drawing on his experience as a fourth-generation Australian furniture maker and a graduate of the Australian National University School of Art & Design. His work has been exhibited around the world and collected by major museums. He sees Australia as naturally growing its own aesthetic and personality, and most of his work is focused on commissions and limited-edition pieces. 'It's my whole ethos that it will be collected and cherished and loved,' he says.

Narrabundah
House

+ S1 screen

ARCHITECT

Light House Architecture & Science

———

DESIGNER

Elliot Bastianon

Artist in the house

A basic house made with a basic mode of construction was the starting point for this newly redesigned home in the Canberra suburb of Narrabundah. The origins of the house lie in a history that is particular to Canberra. When the Australian government of the 1940s and 1950s built housing for public servants, they used a type of prefabricated housing called monocrete, which uses precast concrete slabs. The results may have been efficient in construction time and costs, but unfortunately the material offered little insulation to cope with Canberra's cold winters and hot summers. The artist and owner of Narrabundah House had already lived through several cold winters and hot summers before she contacted Andy Verri (then at Light House Architecture & Science) to help her with an extension and redesign of the house.

Despite its poorly insulated cladding, the house has many appealing design aspects, such as a butterfly roof and high, sloping ceilings with large proportions. Verri worked with the owner to retain and accentuate these modernist design features, while also solving the problem of much-needed insulation with a novel solution: adding a layer of white polystyrene material to the exterior of the house. The extra layer was rendered in white and works with the existing monocrete to create a barrier to the cold (and heat). This solution also allowed the concrete texture of the monocrete (which the owner loved) to be retained inside.

The kitchen is the heart of this modestly proportioned home.

The original monocrete texture was retained inside the house.

The kitchen features simple materials such as recycled blackbutt flooring.

The long handle for the front door was made from a piece of salvaged blackbutt.

The bathroom has views through to the courtyard outside.

While the existing house was rendered in white, the extension is clad in black corrugated iron. It includes a sunken living room, lowered to better connect with the garden, and offers views to the Brindabella Range. The extension is joined to the kitchen, creating a new wing to the house. Opposite this, in the garden, a detached building – also clad in black – was designed as an artist's studio. The master bedroom at the front of the house was extended with an ensuite and walk-in wardrobe, and also has a black exterior. To the right of the front door, a new garage has been built. It has a silver exterior made with a special galvanised steel mesh that allows views to the outside but blocks views into the garage. This creates a rational order to the house – at the front door, the left side is black, the right is silver and the corridor straight ahead is clad in white. Andy Verri describes the design of a house as 'the exploration of a journey. It's not a quick fix, it's a slow-cooked meal. The ingredients are energy efficiency, comfort, light. Spices are added at the end, like materials in a house – stone or timber. They give it taste and flavour.'

With a focus on insulation for energy efficiency, this modestly proportioned house emphasises quality over quantity and simple materials over flashy design details.

With a focus on insulation for energy efficiency, this modestly proportioned house emphasises quality over quantity and simple materials over flashy design details. The materials palette includes natural honed bluestone tiling, polished concrete slab and recycled blackbutt flooring. LED strip lighting throughout and integrated joinery also add to the sense of an integrated design solution. The heroes in the house are the owner's collection of paintings, ceramics and objects, including the S1 screen by local Canberra designer Elliot Bastianon. The owner purchased the piece after meeting Bastianon during the DESIGN Canberra Festival, where the screen was featured as part of a focus on local design. Made from recycled felt and timber, the S1 screen sits perfectly alongside the material choices of the house. A bespoke handle for the front door, designed by Verri, was made from a beautiful piece of blackbutt timber that the owner salvaged and had been keeping in her car. The focus here is on creating an energy-efficient house that is not oversized, but is perfect for the owner and how she wants to live, and gives her art collection pride of place.

⌃ The sunken living room connects with the kitchen and dining space.

⟨ Aria Stone's *Light Blue* rests behind a collection of glassware in similar colours.

⟪ Ceramics, objects and artworks from the owner's collection.

NARRABUNDAH HOUSE

LOCATION
Narrabundah, Australian Capital Territory

————

DETAILS
House; 3 bedrooms,
2 bathrooms; 172 m²

————

ARCHITECT
Light House Architecture & Science

————

BUILDER
Jigsaw Housing

————

PHOTOGRAPHY
Ben Wrigley and Rod Vargas

∨ The artist's studio, clad in
black, is detached from the
rest of the house.

Material exploration

Elliot Bastianon grew up on the north coast of New South Wales but moved to Canberra to study furniture at the Australian National University School of Art & Design. At the time, it was one of the only schools offering furniture making as an art, with a craft focus. His studies were highly influential, laying the groundwork for thinking outside the box when it comes to materials. The S1 screen is the result of his honours-year exploration into EchoPanel, a recycled felt-like material, and its possibilities for use as a primary material in the construction of furniture and lighting. His experiments with the material, which has unique qualities (it absorbs sound and is quite rigid, despite being textile-like), led to a series of designs, not all of which were 100 per cent successful. While sometimes frustrating to work with, the material limitation Bastianon set for himself ended up proving fruitful.

The S1 screen was one of the most successful designs to come from this material. The felt is held in a stripped-back timber frame, creating a traditional screen – a type of furniture not often explored by contemporary furniture designers. 'A lot of designers are tripping over themselves to make a chair, but a screen is a forgotten genre of furniture,' says Bastianon. Small spaces mean more people living in close proximity, with a potential need for privacy, he argues. The felt's geometry is simple but effective, and it creates a beautiful and contemporary aesthetic for residential use.

S1 SCREEN

DESIGNER
Elliot Bastianon

—

MATERIALS
EchoPanel, Victorian ash

—

DETAILS OF CONSTRUCTION/MAKING
Mortice and tenon joinery, scored and folded acoustic panelling

—

PHOTOGRAPHY
David Lindesay

Fitzroy Loft

+ Tidal lounger

ARCHITECT
Architects EAT

—

DESIGNER
Trent Jansen

Refining the box

This home proves that not all outstanding Australian architecture has to have a backyard or a water view. Situated in a converted 1890s warehouse that was once the MacRobertson chocolate factory, then an Aikido Dojo martial arts studio and an advertising agency before being converted to residential use in the 1990s, this space featured beautiful high ceilings, but the charm of its original industrial heritage was gone when Albert Mo from Architects EAT first came to it. 'Over time, it had been degraded to become something quite ordinary,' explains Mo. That is, until they started to demolish the internal finishes of the space to uncover what lay beneath.

Luckily, the architects' office was just around the corner, so whenever something interesting was uncovered during the demolition process, the builders would call the architects and ask when and where to stop. As the layers were peeled back, a number of features were exposed, including original paintwork, brick walls and beautiful timber trusses that had previously been hidden above the ceiling. 'One of the most exciting moments was when an old sign saying "Fire alarm" was uncovered. I said, "Stop everything", and we came over and wrapped it up to protect it.'

The charm of these original features was retained in the final home – a spacious four-bedroom loft – and contrasted with new finishes to create a distinctive aesthetic. In particular, the architecture team was keen to make sure that the space kept its industrial aesthetic as much as possible, while also feeling luxurious

∧ The window seat in the living room creates flexibility for socialising.

< The building's original features were uncovered when the ceiling was removed.

> Vertical lines and light-coloured finishes provide visual interest in the kitchen.

∨ The large, open living space has ceilings of different heights.

and timeless. One of the most important aspects of a warehouse feel is the ceiling height, so the space planning had to take this into consideration. Consequently, the design approach was to create a mezzanine layer across some, but not all, of the interiors, retaining three double-height voids to bring in light and create a sense of volume, while offering more floor space through two insertions that act almost like boxes within a box. This strategy increased the footprint of the interiors from 250 to 400 square metres.

Probably the most significant of these voids is in the courtyard – an external space that was previously enclosed and is now open to the elements via a sloping mesh roof. The walls were left largely untouched, with peeling paint recalling the building's industrial past, while green turf underfoot, plants, outdoor lighting and classic Australian outdoor furniture, such as the Tidal seat and table, combine to reinforce a feeling of being outdoors.

The entry is through a corridor that runs beside the courtyard, separated by a wall of glass framed in black. This corridor continues behind the kitchen until you reach the main living space. There is no formal threshold where the courtyard and the living room meet – the work of distinguishing indoor and outdoor is done by the finishes themselves rather than a change in level. A window seat has been installed here, both inside and out, offering a flexible space for people to sit together and socialise, or simply contemplate the world.

∧ The suspension bridge casts patterned shadows in a patch of sunlight.

⌐ New tiling in the bathroom surrounds an existing piece of wall.

› Flaking paint on beams and old brickwork combine with steel to create an industrial aesthetic.

Inside, the living space and kitchen feature a low ceiling, but this opens up into another double-height void that gives a sense of volume, light and air above the dining room. Heading through a second living space, also with a low ceiling, you come to a third void in the library, which features a double-height wall of books and a ladder to reach them.

Upstairs, the master bedroom and ensuite on one side and two bedrooms with a study on the other are linked by an engineered suspension bridge that tightens as you walk out onto it. 'A bridge is something that all architects dream of doing,' enthuses Mo, who worked closely with the engineer and the builder to make it happen. The metal finish of the bridge harkens back to the industrial history of the warehouse. This finish is repeated in the study on this floor, in the form of a spiral staircase, and throughout the apartment's steel windows and doors. Despite this, the domestic quality of the interiors is not diminished. These interiors are not overtly harsh or mechanical. Instead, flaking paint on beams, old brickwork, grey timber and soft furnishings create a warehouse conversion that is warm, inviting and presents a connection to the outdoors within an urban context.

"A bridge is something that all architects dream of doing."

— Albert Mo

> The second double-height void is lined with a wall of books and a ladder for accessing them.

∨ The cables of the suspension bridge tighten as you walk across.

The bedroom connects to the bathroom and overlooks the courtyard.

The bathroom is finished in a mix of old and new materials.

The bedroom features a sloping ceiling and exposed timber trusses.

FITZROY LOFT

LOCATION
Fitzroy, Victoria

——

DETAILS
Factory conversion; 4 bedrooms,
3 bathrooms; 400 m²

——

ARCHITECT
Architects EAT

——

BUILDER
Guild

——

PHOTOGRAPHY
Derek Swalwell

∧ Steel is the material of choice for
the spiral staircase in the study.

Riding a wave of nostalgia

TIDAL LOUNGER

DESIGNER
Trent Jansen

———

MATERIALS
Stainless steel, glass, porcelain, outdoor
foam and outdoor textile

———

DETAILS OF CONSTRUCTION/MAKING
CNC wire bent and welded frame
with upholstered cushion

———

BRAND/MANUFACTURER
Tait

———

PHOTOGRAPHY
Albert Comper

Sydney designer Trent Jansen designed Tidal – an outdoor lounger chair and coffee table – for Melbourne outdoor furniture brand Tait. The brief asked for a poolside collection that referenced Australian beach nostalgia. Jansen collected beachside photography from the 1970s and drew inspiration from the fashion, the hairstyles and the bicycles the kids were riding. He also took on an angular aesthetic that transitioned from the mid-century modern to the 1970s, including the Bertoia side chair, which Jansen cites as a huge influence. As a designer for whom research is vital, Jansen also went beyond a merely stylistic approach to investigate a deeper narrative – the science of waves. 'I was looking at the stages of a wave,' he explains. Working with two interns, he started to sketch the forms inspired by these waves. 'These are voluptuous, round forms that reference the water.'

The resulting shapes are distinctly original, neither copying the famous curves of the Bertoia side chair nor settling for a basic geometry common to other outdoor wire furniture. For Jansen, the experience of working with Gordon and Suzie Tait was pivotal to the success of this project. 'Gordon, as a technician with material knowledge and process knowledge, brought a huge amount to the project,' explains Jansen. 'The lounger required a lot of testing that couldn't have happened without him and his staff. They are such a generous and open company.'

The Tidal lounger and coffee table are vital to the Fitzroy Loft project. They create a sense of the outdoors in the courtyard space, while also echoing the black steel of the architecture. When the architects brought the pieces in for the photo shoot, the owners of the loft loved them so much they bought them. 'It's so nice to see your work in a beautiful space,' says Jansen. 'Seeing it being used – where it lives – rather than just in concept or in a showroom – to know that those people are sitting on it and their life is happening with those things? That gives me joy.'

Aldgate House

+ Felix sofa

ARCHITECT

Black Rabbit Architecture + Interiors

—

DESIGNER

Arthur G

Radical reconstruction

In a time when landfill waste is increasingly a problem and the building industry is one of the worst culprits, it is heartening to know that some architects and owners are going out of their way to make sure their house project is a renovation, not a demolition.

When Black Rabbit Architecture + Interiors were first contacted by the owners of Aldgate House in the Adelaide Hills, they were confronted with a building that could easily have been one for the bulldozer – a 1970s cream brick house that was dark, gloomy and in poor condition. The house had been extended, but it was still closed off and boxy, with a living wing at one end and bedrooms off a corridor at the other. Lead architect Sean Humphries says it was 'a pretty nondescript Frankenstein of a house, sitting on a pristine piece of land'. But he knew it had good bones.

The owners, a professional couple with kids, are lovers of design who decided to present their design brief to the architects in an unusual way. They wrote a haiku.

> *Things of stone, wood, glass,*
> *Simple elements, combined*
> *To create a home*

∧ The living room extension follows the downward slope of the site.

< Large windows open the living room up to light and garden views.

The architecture team interpreted this as an emphasis on tactility and a spatial experience. Humphries says, 'They had this innate need for something that was not just different but also passively engaged them. You can walk through the house at different times of day and get a different experience. It's never just a white box.' At the same time, Humphries jokes, the haiku wasn't quite enough information – he also needed to know how many bedrooms they wanted.

In terms of its floor plan, the existing house had been pretty basic: bedrooms up one end, the kitchen, living and dining zones in the centre, and a wing with an additional living space and master bedroom at the other end. The new plan extends the centre of the house into the front garden with a grand new entry, and into the back with a sunken living room that mimics the slope of the site. The resulting living zone dissects the parents' wing from the kids' wing, creating a cross-shaped (or cruciform) plan. The benefits of this approach are myriad, but foremost was the intention to get as much light into the house as possible.

According to Humphries, who has done a lot of projects in the Adelaide Hills, cooling is not a problem, but heating can be. The house was poorly oriented, so the architects cut into the house, removing verandah sections and creating larger openings to bring in the sun. The cladding of the building in black weatherboard was also about absorbing warmth, and created a dramatic contrast against the green backdrop of the site. Steel roof cladding was used because it could wrap seamlessly over the roof, creating a mansard roof detail that literally folds up and over the building.

While the outside of the building is masculine and robust, the interiors had to be inviting. The space was designed with a Scandinavian design aesthetic. The Felix sofa in the sunken living room is Australian, but its brown leather upholstery and the long legs that lift the seat above the ground evoke Nordic minimalism. Oak floorboards were used and then wrapped up the walls. A lot of the lighting was concealed, to create a soft glow. In a few places inside the living space, the hard black edge of the exterior is mimicked in the form of cupboards – behind the kitchen, a black box conceals a butler's pantry, laundry and powder room.

The use of timber for the island bench, floors and wall panelling ties the interiors together.

A long line of skylights fills the living spaces with light.

The kitchen features a black box that conceals a butler's pantry, laundry and powder room.

The ethical considerations of sustainability are paramount in this design, resulting in an exceptional piece of design thinking that is also a lot of fun.

For Humphries, the interiors are just as important as the exteriors. He likes to design 'from the inside out'. Details like joinery and finishes give him as much pleasure as the exterior form. His favourite detail is one he made himself – a cat door like a cartoon mouse hole that interrupts the skirting board, giving the cat access to the next room. Humphries made this using materials from the skip, including aluminium trim, pieces of weatherboard and flashing, saving them from landfill in a spirit of make-do.

The ethical considerations of sustainability are paramount in this design, resulting in an exceptional piece of design thinking that is also a lot of fun. 'We felt pretty good about the fact that we didn't have to bulldoze the place. There's so much waste in building as it is. To be able to say, "You know what? This is the right thing to do."'

∧ The second living space incorporates built-in bookshelves and storage.

‹ This interruption in the skirting board allows the cat access between rooms and provides a lovely architectural detail.

‹‹ The white, black and timber palette is also featured in the bathrooms.

∧ Large windows at the back of
the house let in light and provide
views of the garden.

ALDGATE HOUSE

LOCATION
Adelaide Hills, South Australia

——

DETAILS
House; 4 bedrooms and 3 bathrooms
plus powder room; 307 m²

——

ARCHITECT
Black Rabbit Architecture + Interiors

——

BUILDER
Thus

——

LANDSCAPE DESIGNER
Mark Barnett

——

PHOTOGRAPHY
Aaron Citti

Best seat in the house

FELIX SOFA

DESIGNER
Arthur G

———

MATERIALS
Solid Victorian ash frame, high-density premium foam insert, upholstered in Mokum Coupole or leather

———

DETAILS OF CONSTRUCTION/MAKING
Victorian hardwood frame, suspension system, t-junction cushion, saddle-stitched leather

———

PHOTOGRAPHY
Dion Robeson

At Arthur G's Melbourne headquarters, the design and production teams work together to create new ranges of seating, beds, tables and shelving. Established in 1979 by Arthur Georgopoulos, who still works with son and CEO Leonard Georgopoulos, the company sells its designs both to general consumers and to trade via architects and interior designers. All designs are created in-house, apart from a couple of collaborations with independent designers, and manufactured in their large-scale facilities, with all aspects of production located in Australia.

The Felix sofa started with a brief based on the market. When the Felix was designed, much of Arthur G's range was quite boxy and minimal, with heavy designs that reached to the ground. For Felix, they wanted something light, with tall legs that lifted the sofa. They also wanted a particular arm shape that had a bit more character, and a t-junction seat cushion. The aesthetic combined Arthur G's mandate for timeless classic design with a Scandinavian look.

Arthur, Leonard and the design team worked together on the design of Felix, drawing on their expertise to find the best solutions. Starting with a hand-drawn sketch, the design was modelled and made in cardboard before being realised as a prototype to test proportions and ergonomics. This step-by-step process is one that Arthur G has perfected over the last forty years, meaning each piece carries with it a host of knowledge and research and development. In Aldgate House, the Felix sofa and its leather upholstery were selected by the owners and the piece has become a centrepiece of the sunken living room. It brings a masculine warmth that contrasts with the black-and-white palette of this home.

Dalgety Street House

+ Coco
pendant

ARCHITECT
Ha

DESIGNER
Kate Stokes and Coco Flip

The heart of the foodie's home

The kitchen really is the heart of this Melbourne home. Steel-framed windows open up to an urban garden, and a walled deck extends the kitchen and dining room to the outdoors. This Victorian terrace in inner-city St Kilda has been transformed by Nick Harding of Melbourne architecture practice Ha, whose brief from the owner was to bring in light while creating privacy from an adjacent block of apartments. Now a sense of openness and flow extends throughout the house, and enclosed rooms at the front of the house have been opened up, making these living spaces more flexible and light-filled. Harding had a mission to create a clear line of sight from the front door right through to the back. This involved carving into the walls and removing two doors into the ground floor front rooms. All the walls are still there, but they are punctuated by huge openings.

The kitchen is distinctive, with black cabinets and graphic black-and-white floor tiles, and is designed to have a flexible configuration. In winter, opening the steel-framed glass bi-fold doors at the end of the kitchen makes the full-sized pizza oven accessible and brings in crucial northern light, with the small opening keeping out cold air. In warmer weather, the west-facing doors parallel to the dining table can be opened, allowing the dining table to be taken outside for outdoor dining. Alternatively, both sets of doors can be opened up to create freedom of movement across a seamless indoor–outdoor space.

∧ The kitchen's steel-framed bi-fold doors contain windows that open individually.

< Geometric floor tiles and a green splashback bring the black kitchen cabinets to life.

∧ Open bi-fold doors create a seamless transition from the kitchen to the deck.

⌐ Birch trees screen the kitchen and deck from neighbours.

〉 Black lines are echoed in the living room shelving and Halo pendant light.

The walled deck features built-in garden beds and seating nooks, shielding the occupants from the neighbours, while tall birch trees planted on the level below reach up to create another privacy screen. 'We had this idea of creating almost a walled garden which framed the entire kitchen,' explains Harding. 'It's like a huge timber sequence of planter beds that look like they've been chiselled out of this timberwork.'

The black steel frames of the windows in each of the rooms create a graphic language that is repeated throughout the house in the vertical lines of the black kitchen cabinets, the black-and-white tiles on the kitchen floor, the black-framed shelving in the living space and the black circle outline of the living room pendant light, Halo, by Australian designer Christopher Boots. Other finishes include concrete and white marble, with the only real splash of colour entering in the kitchen splashback, which echoes the greenery outside.

The house is situated on a steep slope. The living space and kitchen are on the ground floor at the front of the house, but at the back of the house they form the first floor above a basement bedroom suite where the dark, moody Melbourne colour palette once again reigns. 'We wanted it to be very intimate and warm when you're inside,' explains Harding. 'Dark finishes are more common in Melbourne, without a doubt. It's the climate – it gets cold here in winter and people like the intimacy.'

"We wanted it to be very intimate and warm when you're inside ... Dark finishes are more common in Melbourne, without a doubt. It's the climate – it gets cold here in winter and people like the intimacy."

— Nick Harding

Offering a subtle contrast to the black-and-green palette of the kitchen design is the Coco pendant light by Melbourne designer Kate Stokes. The light features black metal against light brown timber, tying in with the timber dining table and chairs. 'We wanted to have a pendant light that was largeish and creates a lovely downward cast of light over the dining room table,' says Harding.

For Harding and his team, this house was about creating a warm, intimate Melbourne house for an owner who is passionate about food. What they achieved in response to a difficult site is also a delicate balancing act between opening the house up to light and screening it from the neighbours.

< The black steel frames of the windows create a graphic language that is echoed throughout the house with select pieces of lighting and furniture.

The ensuite is connected to the bedroom via a long walk-in wardrobe.

The dark wardrobe joinery blends with the finishes in the rest of the house.

The downstairs bedroom looks out onto a garden of tall birch trees.

DALGETY STREET HOUSE

LOCATION
St Kilda, Victoria

——

DETAILS
Victorian terrace; 3 bedrooms,
3 bathrooms; 282 m²

——

ARCHITECT
Ha

——

BUILDER
Richard Tate Construction

——

PHOTOGRAPHY
Tom Blachford and Kate Ballis

——

STYLIST
Ruth Welsby

∨ Much of the joinery in the house,
including the living room shelves,
was custom-designed.

Juxtaposing metal and timber

COCO PENDANT

DESIGNER
Kate Stokes

———

MATERIALS
Victorian ash, powder-coated aluminium

———

DETAILS OF CONSTRUCTION/MAKING
Hand-turned timber, spun aluminium

———

BRAND/MANUFACTURER
Coco Flip

———

PHOTOGRAPHY
Haydn Cattach

The Coco pendant by Melbourne design studio Coco Flip is so tied to the fortunes of the studio itself that it is often mistakenly referred to as the 'Coco Flip pendant'. Kate Stokes designed the light and launched the studio brand at the same time in 2010. She has received critical acclaim for her design, which took off immediately in the design press worldwide.

The original idea for the light was to combine timber and metal in a seamless way. 'At the time, there weren't many lights around with timber in them,' says Stokes. 'We wanted to create something that had a lot of presence in the room and would hang with ease.' Stokes met with local manufacturers, such as timber turners, early in the process to see what they could do, then worked with her partner, Haslett Grounds, on the 3D-modelling of the piece. The final design is sourced from different makers and packaged up in the studio, twenty at a time.

The Coco pendant – simple, yet proportionally elegant and materially balanced – has become very popular with Australian architects and interior designers, but it is only one of a number of different designs sold by the studio, including several lights and other furniture items. It is fantastic to see the success of this Australian design brand, which has achieved steady growth over the past decade.

Indigo Slam

+ Sunflower chair

ARCHITECT
Smart Design Studio

—

DESIGNER
Khai Liew

Sculptural, monumental, remarkable

Situated on a narrow street in the inner-city suburb of Chippendale, in Sydney, Indigo Slam is instantly recognisable as a significant piece of architecture. Taking up the entire width of the block, its concrete facade curls and folds over three storeys, creating a monumental and highly sculptural presence. The copper gate features the name of the house as a cutaway portion of its vertical rails, while a sculptural water feature hints at this house's connection to – and appreciation of – art.

Designed by William Smart and the team from Smart Design Studio, this house is home to Judith Neilson, art collector, gallerist and one of Australia's wealthiest women. It was Neilson who came up with the name of the house – a reference to a pulp fiction book that she liked the sound of (but still hasn't read). Her brief for the house, apart from the name, included that it must be a place where she could entertain and hold functions and have a dining table for sixty on the ground floor. It had to be a house for her to live in on her own, but also be able to receive her family and friends as guests. It must last 100 years, and it must have no curtains.

Smart and his team designed the house to receive art, creating spaces for specific works and opportunities to show art. 'The other layer to that question is, "What is art and what is architecture and how do you blur the lines?"' says Smart. 'I think I might have said once it was intended as a piece of sculpture to live in, and it's true that every room has a kind of sculptural quality.'

∧ Light plays on the white curves above the staircase.

< The main staircase dominates the huge hall.

∧ Different geometries connect in the sculptural concrete facade.

⌐ The round entry hall has an intimate scale.

⟩ A sixty-seat dining table and operable doors on the ground floor double as a semi-public function space.

The sculptural nature of the facade was inspired by the work of Portuguese architect Álvaro Siza and Spanish sculptor Eduardo Chillida. It is made of in situ concrete supported by steel mullions, and its forms are determined by aesthetic considerations of form and proportion, balanced by architectural calculations about how light enters the building and how these shapes create different spatial qualities. On the facade, each shape has a purpose: the lower curve creates shade for the dining room, the middle shape is a partly covered balcony and the top shape is a light scoop that brings soft light into the top floor. It took Smart a long time to feel happy with the shape. He remembers being in Perth and meeting with his father at a crucial point of the design. 'I'd been drawing at three in the morning and had stuck the drawings up around the room like a madman.'

Inside, the same shapes continue, playing with form and light. The natural light in the house reflects off various surfaces, creating a soft glow. You enter into a circular entry hall with a low ceiling, before passing into the main three-storey atrium with its grand staircase and 14-metre-high ceiling. This is a monumental room that recalls an art gallery or a church. The ground level is given over to a semi-public function space, with operable walls as a series of doors that swing open or shut. They can be used to close off the sixty-seat dining table from the entry foyer and grand staircase, or kept open, depending on the occasion or time of day.

On the facade, each shape has a purpose: the lower curve creates shade for the dining room, the middle shape is a partly covered balcony and the top shape is a light scoop that brings soft light into the top floor.

∧ In the basement, a whiskey cellar features a brickwork ceiling made of four self-supporting square domes.

⌐ Surfaces within the house reflect light in different ways.

> A spacious galley kitchen runs parallel to the dining area.

The floor is locally sourced brick that has a very subtle pink tinge to it, laid precisely in a variety of patterns. Finishes and details are meticulously attended to: the stair rail is in cast brass with a white leather-stitched finish; the metal grate is a thing of beauty; and the windows and blinds are operated by hand, with winders designed by the architects, and the name of the house inlaid. The finishes on the floors and walls have been waxed rather than painted. Everything has been designed to last a century.

Level one has four bedrooms and four bathrooms for Neilson and her guests, furnished with beds, chairs, rugs and lamps, and built-in cupboards. Upstairs, the living space features another dining table that seats twenty, a sitting area and a long, immaculate kitchen, and a small study looks over the stairs and offers an intimate space for respite from the grand halls. The house is full of these changes of scale – from large to small and back again. In the basement is a cave-like cellar that includes an intimate setting where Neilson can drink whiskey with her friends. The cellar's ceiling consists of four self-supporting square-based domes laid in brick – an architectural detail that speaks to the immensity of this house's architectural achievement.

Finishes and details are meticulously attended to: the stair rail is in cast brass with a white leather-stitched finish ... the windows and blinds are operated by hand, with winders designed by the architects ...

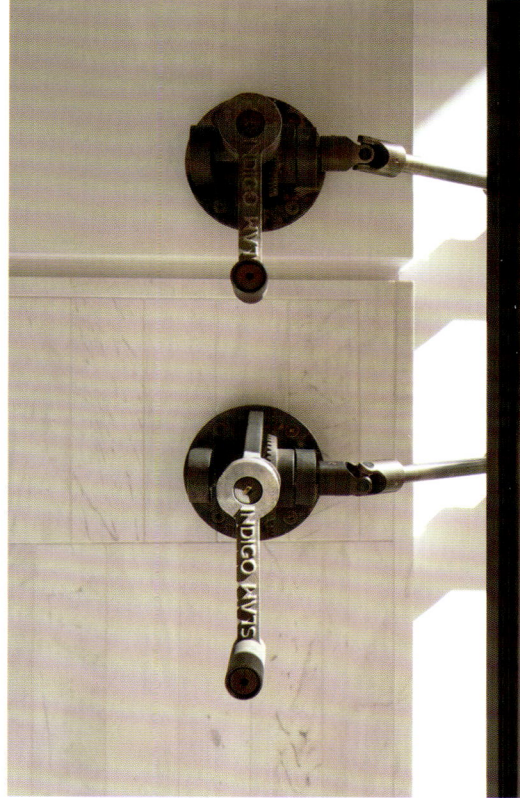

If the detailing of the house is immaculate, the furniture, lighting and rugs are too – this is the incredible achievement of Adelaide-based furniture designer Khai Liew. He and his team of eight worked for four years to design and make 109 key pieces, using over thirty different artisans (including guilders, upholsterers and metal fabricators) to get the right detailing and realise both the owner's and the architecture team's vision. Each piece is designed for its particular place in the house. The Sunflower chair, for example, two of which have been made for the living room on the top floor, offers a sculptural yet comfortable seat whose proportions match the surrounding space, complementing two other armchairs, a sofa, a coffee table and a rug in that particular space. Proportions of furniture are vital, and each one sits in perfect harmony within the whole.

This house is an outstanding achievement. In focusing on the longevity of the building, William Smart and the team at Smart Design Studio, along with all of their collaborators, have positioned Indigo Slam as a monument that Sydneysiders can be proud of for generations to come.

∧ The architects designed the customised window levers.

⌐ Stair rails are cast in brass and finished in white hand-stitched leather.

‹ All the furniture in the house, including the Sunflower chair, was designed by Adelaide's Khai Liew.

∧ The guest rooms on the first level
are filled with bespoke furniture,
rugs and artwork.

〉 A vertical cut in the wall of
the master bathroom lets in
light and allows views out.

〉〉 The master bedroom features
a four-poster bed, a desk and
other design pieces.

INDIGO SLAM

LOCATION
Chippendale, New South Wales

———

DETAILS
House; 4 bedrooms, 4 bathrooms,
2 powder rooms; 1344 m²

———

ARCHITECT
Smart Design Studio

———

BUILDER
Total Coordination

———

PHOTOGRAPHY
Sharrin Rees, David Roche
and Rowena Moore

Floral bloom

SUNFLOWER CHAIR

DESIGNER
Khai Liew

———

MATERIALS
European oak

———

DETAILS OF CONSTRUCTION/MAKING
Handcrafted timber

———

PHOTOGRAPHY
Grant Hancock

Adelaide designer Khai Liew was commissioned by Judith Neilson, the owner of Indigo Slam, to design and make 109 key pieces of furniture, lighting and rugs for her house. This makes it a unique project, not only in Australia but in the world. Liew cites the last commission of this size being when New York governor Nelson Rockefeller sought out furniture designer George Nakashima in 1973 to make a couple of hundred pieces for one of his houses.

Liew's involvement in Indigo Slam started from the very beginning of the project, before Neilson even bought the site. He worked closely with Smart Design Studio to create a series of design objects that made the architecture into a home. This was especially important in such a large house, as the furnishings needed to blend with the architecture and create a sense of flow and continuity.

Liew has many strings to his bow. At his furniture studio in Adelaide, he employs some of the best cabinet-makers in the country, three of whom have been working as cabinet-makers for twenty-five to thirty years. The rest are from Adelaide's home of craft, the Jam Factory, so the level of craftsmanship is high. As well as designing furniture, he also designs houses, is an artist, curator, conservator and building restorer, and in a former life was an antique dealer with an eye for Australian colonial furniture.

His practice continues the impressive level of quality that can be found in Australia's early colonial furniture, but with a completely contemporary aesthetic. The Sunflower chair is a particularly interesting item that created a challenge for Liew's studio and tested his cabinet-makers. 'When I first showed them the design, they obviously went berserk,' he confesses. The trick was to find the balance between strength and fragility in the flower-shaped chair, while also creating a chair that is sturdy and comfortable. For Liew, the design is joyful and expressive, but also warm, thanks to the European oak.

The beauty of Liew's work rests with its quality as well as its aesthetics. This is a conscious choice – and one that has reaped rewards for him and his team. For Australia to compete in terms of making furniture, he insists that we must make finely crafted things that speak of place and time. Indigo Slam and the furniture within it will no doubt be remembered as a pivotal moment in the history of 21st-century Australian design.

Project Zero

+ Snowi
pendant

ARCHITECT

BVN

—

DESIGNER

Jouni Järvelä and Pop Plus

Zero-energy ambitions

Project Zero is not only the name of this Brisbane house, it also articulates its ambition – that the house should produce as much energy as it uses, and that this should be easy to measure and track. The goal was set by the owner/builder, who wanted not only to build his own family home but also to create a prototype for a new, sustainable type of housing in Brisbane. Brian Donovan from architecture firm BVN worked with him from day one, advising on the site before the land was even bought.

The first sustainable choice they made was to work with the existing building – a traditional Queenslander in an inner suburb of Brisbane – rather than razing it and starting again. The second was to completely reimagine the building. Queenslanders are often thought of as ideally designed for their environment because of their wraparound verandahs that block the sun and allow for breezes, but the truth is that their timber construction and corrugated iron roofs do not have any thermal mass, making them cold in winter and hot in summer. Meanwhile, because they are often raised on stumps, their relationship to the garden is not ideal. 'That's, in my mind, one of the classic problems with a Queenslander, having lived here all my life. Very few of them have a positive relationship with the garden,' explains Donovan.

∧ The house was designed to flow seamlessly out to the central garden.

< The kitchen is situated in the new, light-filled wing of the house.

The courtyard is enclosed ... making this a completely private garden space, with turf in the centre for the kids to play on, a 'wild' garden to the side and a pool tucked in behind the garage.

⌐ Clad in brick and concrete, this outdoor room creates a second living space.

› A creeping plant at second-storey height frames the garden.

The building was moved from its existing position to the back of the site and was also turned 90 degrees. A retaining wall in the garden brings the ground level up, so the house is on the same level as the garden. A completely new wing of the house was built along the western edge of the site to create an L shape. This new wing is a single-level brick building with a saw-tooth roof. The brick is actually a much better insulator than the timber of the original house and the new wing was completely built with rejected bricks from the brickyard. The saw-tooth roof has two functions: one side of each ridge faces north to get the best sun for the solar panels, and the other side has vertical windows that bring soft, diffuse, southern light into the interiors. This part of the house features large, open living spaces, including an open-plan kitchen. It all opens directly onto a courtyard garden formed by the L shape of the building.

The courtyard is enclosed on the other side by a garage and at the front by fencing, making this a completely private garden space, with turf in the centre for the kids to play on, a 'wild' garden to the side and a pool tucked in behind the garage. The central courtyard is surrounded by a trellis at second-storey height, with timber palings that are gradually being taken over by a beautiful creeper. Eventually, this timber will be a green halo for this courtyard – a simple idea that creates a beautiful feature for the house.

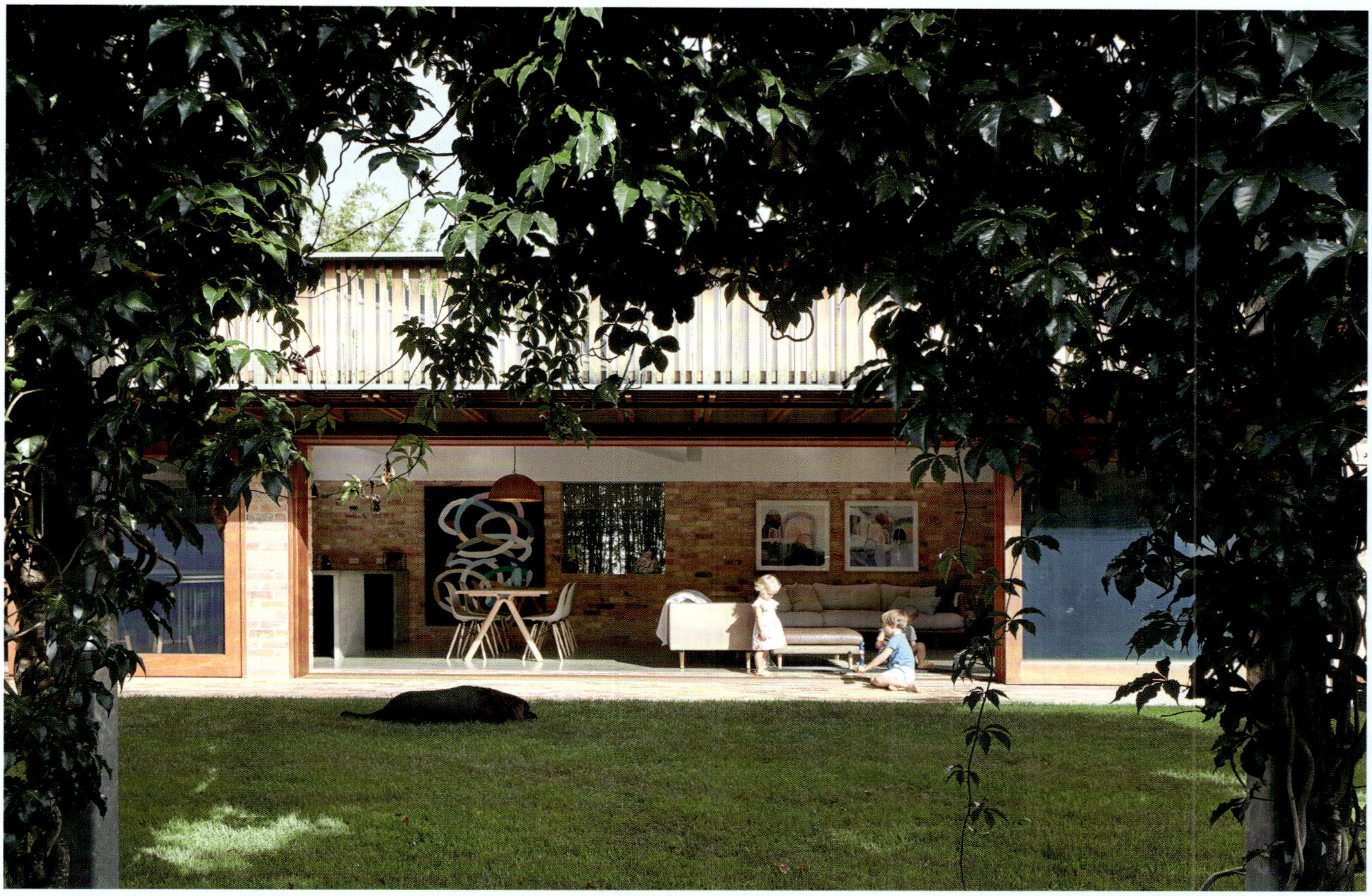

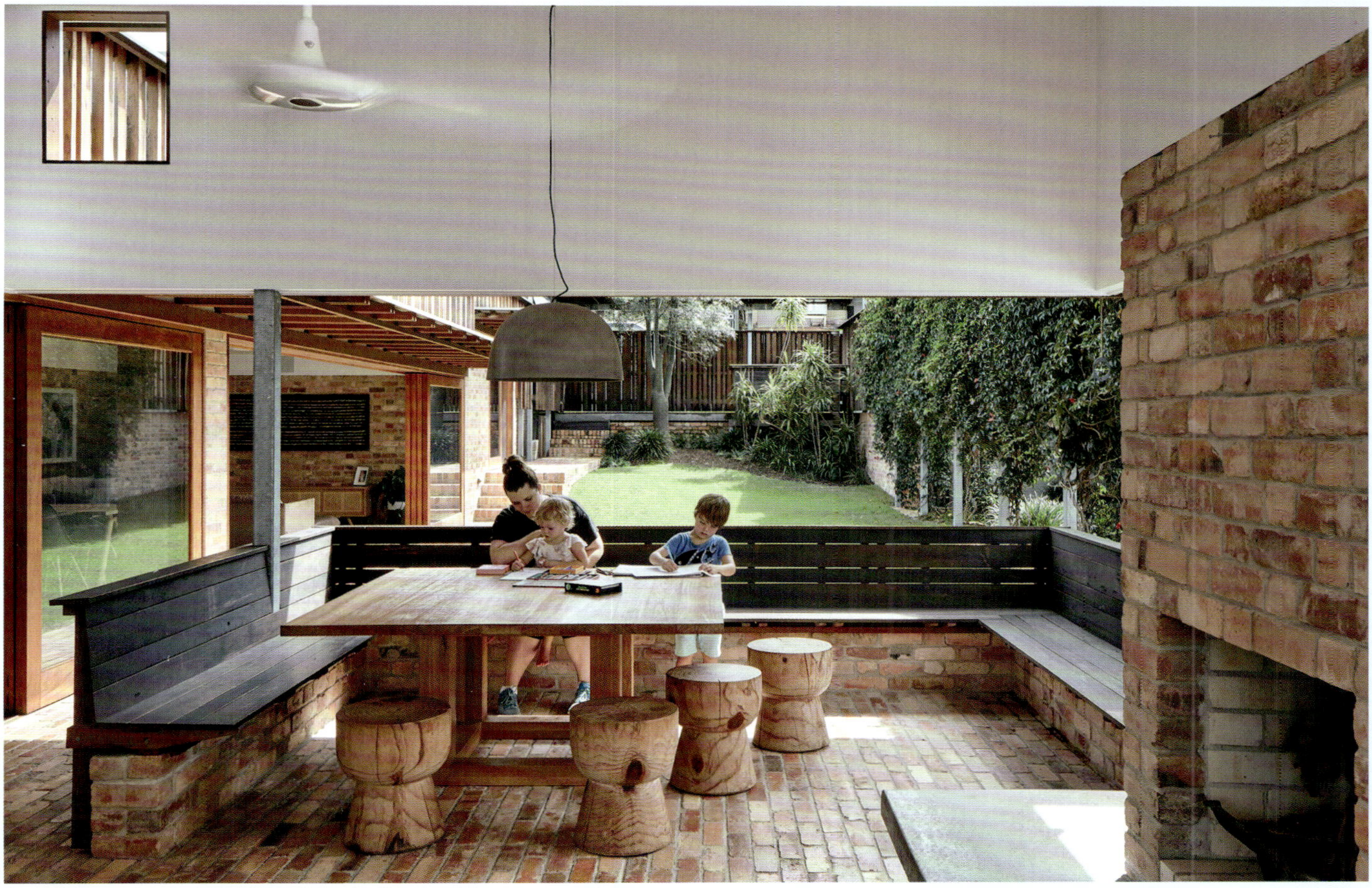

Where the old and new buildings join, another feature of this house has been built – an outdoor room. Clad in brick with built-in seating, it features a huge brick fireplace and brick floors. There is minimal furniture, but it does have a stunning concrete Snowi pendant light, designed by Pop Plus. The entire effect is grounded – the brick and concrete come from the earth and connect to the garden on the same level outside. 'What's terrific about the concrete in the bench and the light is that the natural quality of those materials matches perfectly the natural qualities of the house,' says Donovan.

Bricks are not part of Brisbane's heritage, but they are incredibly sustainable and add thermal mass to this building. The overall selection of materials has been similarly sensitively chosen to get the best sustainable outcome. The rest of the house has also been fitted out with the latest in sustainable technology, including solar heating, water collection, minimum-energy devices and the all-important tracking of energy use. The result is a house that can serve as an example to other Brisbane architects and builders looking to design sustainably. And this prototype has been such a success that the owners are staying put.

∧ The living room opens directly onto the garden via large s iding doors.

⌐ A large brick fireplace makes this outdoor living space usable all year round.

< The extension, with its saw-tooth roof, sits near the perimeter of the site.

∧ The creeper frames a view into the 'wild' part of the garden.

PROJECT ZERO

LOCATION
Alderley, Queensland

———

DETAILS
House; 3 bedrooms,
2 bathrooms; 237 m²

———

ARCHITECT
BVN

———

BUILDER
Apollo Property Group

———

PHOTOGRAPHY
Christopher Frederick Jones

Defying gravity

SNOWI PENDANT

DESIGNER
Jouni Järvelä

———

MATERIALS
Concrete, cloth cord, acrylic diffuser

———

DETAILS OF CONSTRUCTION/MAKING
Off-form exterior, hand-finished interior

———

BRAND/MANUFACTURER
Pop Plus

———

PHOTOGRAPHY
Courtesy of Pop Plus

Jouni Järvelä has always worked with concrete. One of three brothers, Järvelä worked with his brothers and father in concrete construction before they closed what was a physically demanding business to explore other avenues. Järvelä studied industrial and product design at university, exploring a range of materials and learning about his Finnish heritage and the design heritage of Finland. All the different strands of his life came together when he and his brother Sami set up Pop Concrete in Brisbane, offering everything from kitchen benchtops to cafe fit-outs, all in concrete. An arm of the business, Pop Plus, was set up to explore concrete products including lighting, benches, chairs, tables and other furniture pieces.

Knowing concrete so well has helped Järvelä overcome some of the challenges of working with the material. He works with a concrete mix that contains glass fibres to strengthen it and make it lighter. His love of concrete shows in pieces that look as natural as possible, recalling the earthy origins of the material. The Snowi pendant light is one of these pieces. The faceted surface of the shade is created from a fibreglass mould, while the internal part of the light is hand-finished. 'You can still see the strokes of the hand from how it was manufactured,' Järvelä explains. The dome shape of the Snowi light is a strong shape in itself, which means its shell can be thin. The light looks weighty, like concrete, but also manages to float in midair.

Allen Key House

+HB table

ARCHITECT
Studio Prineas

—

DESIGNER
Russel Koskela

Simplicity is not the same as simple

This suburban house in Sydney's Lower North Shore once had a rickety deck out the back. Despite its dilapidated condition, it was a favourite place where meals were eaten outside, overlooking the garden. Still the focal point of this family house, the old lean-to and deck were demolished and replaced with an expansive living room and a kitchen with high ceilings. This opens what was a poky back deck on a 1930s Californian bungalow into a contemporary space for family living.

The brief for architect Eva-Marie Prineas and her team was to create a functional house for a small family, without blowing the modest budget set by the owners. As a result, the new extension was designed on a grid determined by the size of Ikea flat-pack furniture. Prineas explains, 'We said to them, "We can do it for this budget, but you have to be happy with Ikea." Most people wouldn't put the effort in, but they went off and bought it all. There were bits of modification required but basically, we set it up on that grid.' Due to the importance of the flat-pack in the architect's design, the project was dubbed the 'Allen Key House'.

Another vital aspect of this design was to bring light right in to the centre of the house. Where the old house transitions to the new addition, two internal courtyards have been created on either side of the central thoroughfare. They serve as light wells, bringing light and ventilation to two existing rooms (one ensuite bathroom and one study space) and into the new section of the house.

⌃ The kitchen splashback was replaced with windows to bring greenery inside.

⟨ The generously proportioned living room is the focal point of the house.

⟩ The living area is large, open and light, with views onto leafy exteriors.

∧ The simple, white kitchen has a concrete floor and black details.

⌐ Russel Koskela's HB table, with black-stained legs, is the centrepiece of the dining area.

> The kitchen's ceiling is raised by dormer-style windows.

A new master bedroom, with an adjoining ensuite and walk-in wardrobe, on one side, and a study plus laundry (with outside access) on the other, create functional spaces for contemporary living, replacing the tiny kitchen and dining room that were previously here. From this point, the house opens up to the main living space, with its generous proportions. Oversized dormer-style windows create extra height above the kitchen and dining room areas and in the living space. The resulting room is one big shed-like space whose shape has been manipulated at the ceiling plane to bring in natural light. The changing ceiling heights give a sense of separate zones within the expanse.

By bringing the width of the house in on only one side, the ridge line of the roof – central in the front part of the house – becomes asymmetrical in the back portion of the house, creating a raked ceiling and also lending a fantastic geometry to the exterior profile. The colour palette is kept very simple – all white to match the flat-pack joinery, with outlines in black on the windows and some details to highlight the shapes of openings.

Windows in the kitchen are placed where the splashback would normally be, creating a picture window that opens onto greenery. Windows above the kitchen cupboards bring light into the room above normal ceiling height, while those in the dining space are at ground level and also reach up to what feels almost like a double-height void, again offering views of greenery outside.

For Prineas and her team, these portals were created specifically to bring the leafy garden into the house – almost like picture frames to a jungle scene outside.

In addition to the simplicity and affordability of the finishes – including polished concrete floor slabs finished in matte satin polyurethane and black aluminium window frames – the clients invested in a few key pieces, which stand out against the neutral palette in warm timber and subtle colours. The HB table by Sydney furniture designer Russel Koskela features a clear outline of black legs against timber that perfectly echoes the black outlines in the interiors and architecture that surround it.

This project is not about achieving status through the latest must-have details. People think that if they buy *this* benchtop or *that* light, it will look the same as it does in a magazine, but Prineas insists that it's not about that. 'When people look at this project, they look at the space and the windows and they can't believe the volume,' she says. The new design proves not only that simplicity is sometimes more beautiful but also that it's not just people with unusually deep pockets who can afford to live in an architect-designed home.

∧ The large window in the bathroom opens onto an internal courtyard.

⌐ The bathroom design does not focus on expensive finishes or fittings, but on flooding the space with light.

< Bedrooms in the existing part of the house have been kept simple.

ALLEN KEY HOUSE

LOCATION
Lane Cove, New South Wales

———

DETAILS
Californian bungalow; 4 bedrooms,
2 bathrooms; 220 m²

———

ARCHITECT
Studio Prineas

———

BUILDER
Element Constructions

———

PHOTOGRAPHY
Chris Warnes

⌃ A new internal courtyard brings
light into the study space.

I'll pencil you in

HB TABLE

DESIGNER
Russel Koskela

MATERIALS
Veneer white ash top, solid American white
ash (lime-washed or black-stained) legs

DETAILS OF CONSTRUCTION/MAKING
Solid timber joinery base

BRAND/MANUFACTURER
Koskela

PHOTOGRAPHY
Macarena Whittle

When Russel Koskela and his wife, Sasha Titchkosky, started their
Australian furniture business eighteen years ago, they were advised
by many that the furniture industry was being taken over by
China, that everyone would be buying furniture on the internet
and that people wouldn't pay the prices needed to manufacture
locally. Luckily, they ignored that advice. Koskela (the brand) began
by selling a small range of furniture designed by Russel and
made by local manufacturers. It quickly took off, with orders of
hundreds of pieces per project proving that there was a market
for Australian-designed furniture in Sydney.

    Since then, the brand has grown from strength to strength,
selling not only work designed by Russel and his team of designers
but also work designed by other Sydneysiders. Now based in an old
canning factory in the semi-industrial suburb of Rosebery, Koskela
offers a range of furniture, lighting, rugs, homewares, books and
gifts, accompanied by a cafe and situated in a precinct synonymous
with design and good food.

    The HB table was designed by Russel. It is a simple design,
made with light and dark timber veneers, whose legs join at the
extreme ends of the tabletop and connect underneath to form
a rectangular profile. Another piece of timber connects the entire
table along its spine at floor level.

    The most distinctive part of the HB table's design can be
found on the legs, where a bevelled edge has been carved out and
one of the legs has been branded 'Koskela'. This design element was
inspired by Russel's childhood memories. 'If you didn't want other
kids to steal your pencil, you could chew it or you could carve into
the end of the pencil and write your name on it,' he says. Russel and
his team experimented with carving the leg in the same way, and
the result is the HB table – named after the type of pencil Russel
remembers using.

    The HB table was suggested by architect Eva-Marie Prineas
for the Allen Key House as a signature piece that was also an
Australian design. 'More people should use an architect and more
people should use Australian furniture,' says Russel. 'Even if it's just
one piece, you treasure it.'

Kew Residence

+ Liqueur table

ARCHITECT
Doherty Design Studio

—

DESIGNER
Ross Didier

Domestic balance

The design of this house in the Melbourne suburb of Kew, for a family who loves to entertain up to eighty people at a time, tempers its oversized proportions through the use of geometric patterns and overlapping and contrasting materials, resulting in a home with balanced proportions that is harmonious, but also has character. The owners invited Doherty Design Studio to design the interiors after admiring another of their projects. They also asked them to design the house itself, which Doherty Design Studio did in consultation with a drafter. The resulting house offers a variety of different living spaces, both inside and out, with carefully curated design details creating a distinctive look and feel.

The exterior facade is broken up into two forms on the left and right, each one featuring white brick cladding surrounding floor-to-ceiling glazing. Slatted timber cladding has been used to break up any sense of a monumental presence. On the left, the garage is entirely clad in timber slats, while the centre of the house is in introverted black with a black decorative mesh screen entry door. This is the first of many geometric decorative moments throughout the house. Inside this entry door, the white brick of the exterior wraps inside and a second front door creates a vestibule. This is clad in timber, with fluted glass and a large square green onyx-and-brass doorhandle. For Mardi Doherty, these details were selected to add a 1930s 'almost Hollywood architecture' resonance.

∧ Stairs link the kitchen and dining area to the sunken living room.

‹ The geometric-patterned black entry door leads to a vestibule clad in white brick.

∧ The green onyx of the kitchen splashback also features in the front doorhandle and bathroom finishes.

❭ The living room opens onto the outdoor courtyard, which can be screened with floor-to-ceiling curtains.

Inside, a long, wide hallway runs from the front door to the kitchen and dining space at the back, with sunken living rooms to the right at the front and rear of the house, and an outdoor courtyard in-between. To the left of the hall, the garage sits at the front. In the middle is a staircase that leads to the bedrooms upstairs. The staircase is enclosed in a black screen with fluted glass, playing on some of the same design features as the entryway. Underneath the stair area is a bar that makes the hallway part of the entertaining space – it is twice as wide as a regular hallway, creating a sense of generous space to the house.

Everything is generous, which meets the needs of a Greek family who entertains once a month or so. The courtyard forms the centre of the space, capturing the northern light, with three sliding doors that can be opened up to the front and rear living spaces and the hallway to create a huge indoor–outdoor room. 'It really revolved around this amazingly vast entertainment area,' explains Doherty. 'Generally, hallways are for moving people from one area to the next, whereas this was part of an expandable entertaining area.'

The green onyx of the front doorhandle carries through to the splashback of the kitchen and to the bathroom, representing another nod to the 1930s. Built-in joinery, part of the client's brief, adds a sense of refined detail to the finishes. This includes not only the kitchen, bathrooms and bedroom joinery, but also a built-in

Inside, a long, wide hallway runs from the front door to the kitchen and dining space at the back, with sunken living rooms to the right at the front and rear of the house, and an outdoor courtyard in-between.

sofa in the sunken living room that adjoins the kitchen and dining space. This was a custom design that was difficult to get right. It had to work in tandem with a mesh screen from the upper level that separates the living areas, and also allows views through from one room to the next.

The design team selected much of the furniture and lighting. Ross Didier's Liqueur table is one of the most important pieces of furniture in the whole house. It is positioned at a focal point within the kitchen, dining and living space at the rear of the house, and it can be viewed for about 30 metres as you walk down the hallway from the front entrance.

With even its hallway being double the width of a standard Victorian house, this property feels generous without losing elegance. The colours and materials centre on a basic palette of neutrals, adding splashes of muted colour in soft furnishings and interest via geometric design elements throughout.

∧ Ross Didier's Liqueur table can be seen at the end of the generously proportioned hallway.

‹ The sunken living room is at the front of the house, just past the entry.

« The Featherston E254 chair and footstool add classic Australian design to the mix.

∧ Bespoke joinery with geometric details adds a level of sophistication to the bedrooms.

> In the bathroom, an asymmetrical mirror sits above black tiles that seem to jump off the bathroom wall.

>> The interiors feature a layering of materials and textures.

‹ Built-in joinery, including desks and storage, creates intimate spaces from functional design.

« Geometries found elsewhere in the house are echoed in the bathroom mirrors and tiles.

⌄ The walk-in wardrobe is tucked behind bedroom joinery that forms an oversized bedhead.

‹ The outdoor entertaining areas
   have seating in neutral colours.

∨ The outdoor path is surrounded
   by greenery.

KEW RESIDENCE

LOCATION
Kew, Victoria

—

DETAILS
House; 4 bedrooms, 3 bathrooms,
1 powder room; 400 m²

—

INTERIOR DESIGNER
Doherty Design Studio

—

DRAFTER
Nassima Design Group

—

BUILDER
Barbat James Homes

—

PHOTOGRAPHY
Derek Swalwell and Alex Reinders

Evolving craft

Ross Didier is a Melbourne-based designer whose furniture and lighting pieces are made as production pieces but still retain a handcrafted aesthetic. He studied industrial design and sculpture at RMIT University then worked in backstage theatre production. His early pieces were expressive and fine art–directed, before he started working with international brands like Allermuir on furniture pieces. Now he is working on small batch production made in his own workshop.

For Didier, there is an added challenge of what he calls the 'rational part' of the design process: getting the ergonomics right, getting the strength right, making sure it lasts for the purpose it was made for and, lastly, making it affordable. 'If fine art is bare-knuckle fighting, then design is Shaolin Kung Fu,' Didier says.

The Liqueur table was designed as an evolution of Didier's Elfin stool, which was made with a construction inspired by the wine barrel. The Liqueur table is constructed in the same way but features an elliptical tabletop. It looks like it could be made by hand, but it is actually engineered as a production piece – with all the design modifications that this requires – and made to last in solid American oak.

LIQUEUR TABLE

DESIGNER
Ross Didier

MATERIALS
American oak (optional veneer or laminate), steel plate

DETAILS OF CONSTRUCTION/MAKING
Base pedestals fabricated with tapered staves; tabletop options include round tops on a single base, and elliptical or rectangular tops supported on twin pedestals

PHOTOGRAPHY
Michael Kai

Untitled 06

+ Sway lamp

ARCHITECT
Bagnoli Architects

—

DESIGNER
Nick Rennie

Architecture of surprise

This home in the Melbourne suburb of Hawthorn has been designed with a spirit of playfulness. Collaborating with the owners – a builder and a furniture manufacturer – architect Stefan Bagnoli has created a building that defies expectations. Part of this was about creating moments of surprise that invite interaction: a place to sit, a view through a portal, a stopping place to view a piece of art. The house also features forms reminiscent of a children's storybook, secret doors through wardrobes and a dog run underneath the floor.

What sets this house apart is the way the first-floor addition has been designed, especially its relationship to the ground floor. In a playful nod to children's drawings, the upper storey features a pitched roof in a blocky style with a strong silhouette – the whole storey looks almost like a building block has been placed on top of the house from above by a giant hand. Clad in timber and zinc, the upper storey also features timber screening over the windows to accentuate its monolithic shape. The three parts of the roofline are slightly offset, so that you get unusual junctions both outside and in. But what really creates the illusion of the building block shape is the way the upper storey is slightly off-centre from the ground floor. 'It is quite lopsided,' says Bagnoli. 'The idea is that it feels like it's going to fall off. It's just sort of perched up there.'

⌃ On the ground floor, steel and glass are used at the building's edges, creating transparency.

‹ The entry leads to the kitchen and dining space, and upstairs via a spiral staircase.

Downstairs, the edges of the building dissolve, with steel and glass at its fringes creating transparency at the corners of the house. Vertical walls that act as gallery spaces for artwork can be seen throughout the ground-storey living areas, with the vertical accentuated so they seem like they are floating. A series of columns near the back door are off-centre and non-load-bearing, offering another sense of being off-balance and creating a playful breakdown of the usual (sometimes boring) floor plans common in Australian architecture. This approach is inspired by Italian architect and designer Gio Ponti. 'He made me realise that a plan doesn't have to be beautiful on paper for it to be good in reality. Things look a little odd but it doesn't matter, because when you experience it, you don't experience it as a whole in that way,' says Bagnoli.

Instead of taking an overall view of the design, Bagnoli sees the house as a series of moments that are experienced through living there, such as stopping at a wall to look at an artwork or sitting on the step next to the shoe cupboard to put on your shoes. All of these moments have been designed to be experienced in a certain way. A playful light, the Sway floor lamp, rocks back and forth when you touch it, creating an experiential moment that appeals to the child in us. Other moments are more unexpected, such as a glass strip in the floor running the length of the dining room that reveals an underfloor dog run connecting the front and back yards. The family dog loves it and races along underfoot.

⌃ The ceiling levels of the upstairs hallway shift due to the geometries of the offset roofline.

⌐ Distinctive vertical brass rods enclose the spiral staircase and tie in with the materiality of the kitchen.

⟨ The kitchen features gleaming brass finishes and a sculptural light overhead.

This home in the Melbourne suburb
of Hawthorn has been designed with
a spirit of playfulness ... creating moments
of surprise that invite interaction:
a place to sit, a view through a portal,
a stopping place to view a piece of art.

In the backyard, the fence features palings with three sides, one of which is mirrored to reflect the grass and bring light inside. The bathroom is hidden by joinery and has a huge skylight, so you open the door expecting a dark space and instead get one that's filled with light. Above the front study is a mezzanine space that can be accessed from a cupboard in the room below, or from a hatch in the bedroom, like a secret door in a storybook castle. Another hidden door from the upstairs bedroom cupboard leads to the roof deck. 'It's an experimental house,' says Bagnoli. 'You've got these secret passages – it's a bit *The Lion, the Witch and the Wardrobe.*'

In some ways, this house renovation and addition is much like many others in Australia – it retains the front facade, extends to the side and rear and adds a first floor. It increases the bedrooms from two to three, plus a study. It maximises natural light. It hides storage, bathrooms and more behind joinery. But the approach to this most common of architectural projects in Australia – the renovation of and addition to a Victorian terrace – is uncommon. Thanks to an unconventional approach that's full of joy, it doesn't matter what the house looks like in plan – only how it feels as it is experienced moment to moment.

∧ The window seat in the bedroom offers storage as well as a place to sit.

‹ Slats outside the bathroom windows cast long shadows.

« The bathroom uses the same metallic finish as the kitchen, and mosaic tiles.

UNTITLED 06

LOCATION
Hawthorn, Victoria

——

DETAILS
House; 3 bedrooms,
3 bathrooms; 200 m²

——

ARCHITECT
Bagnoli Architects

——

BUILDER
Seventy7 Projects

——

PHOTOGRAPHY
Peter Bennetts

∨ The unexpected design elements
of the exterior include a
lopsided upper level and slender
supporting columns.

Design in motion

A playful design for a playful house, Sway, designed by Melbourne-based Nick Rennie, is a floor lamp that rocks back and forth when it is bumped or pushed. This is not the first interactive design by Rennie, whose Rocking Mushroom Lamp was launched with French brand Ligne Roset in 2014. However, it does mark a new phase in his career of working with Australian manufacturers who are enjoying unprecedented success. In one year, Rennie launched more products manufactured in Australia than he had launched with European manufacturers in the previous sixteen years.

One of these Australian manufacturers is Made by Pen, a Melbourne-based business that currently has five products on the market and whose co-founders are the owners of this house. The initial brief from Made by Pen's owners to Nick Rennie for the Sway lamp was simple – to create a portable floor lamp. It was Rennie who saw the potential of an interactive design. 'It just screamed out that it needs to have this movement from the rounded base,' says Rennie. 'It's a static object, but it has a life of its own when it's bumped or knocked.' Launched in Paris, the Sway light's design has been refined by Made by Pen's in-house engineers to include functionality like motion sensors, timers and a range of settings. With these technical modifications, the design is not just Australian, it is world-class.

SWAY LAMP

DESIGNER
Nick Rennie

MATERIALS
LED, metal, plastic, silicone, electrics, carbon fibre

DETAILS OF CONSTRUCTION/MAKING
Injection moulding, die-casting, machining

BRAND/MANUFACTURER
Made by Pen

PHOTOGRAPHY
Jonathon Ng, Itsuka Studio

Armadale House

+ Surface Sconce

ARCHITECT

B.E Architecture

—

DESIGNER

Henry Wilson

Granite expression

A house wrapped in 260 tonnes of granite has created a sanctuary for a couple and their collection of artworks and family treasures. The building was designed for a couple with adult children who had done many renovations over the years. This time they wanted a new build that also had the kind of handcrafted charm and character you might find in a heritage property. For this, they turned to B.E Architecture, a studio in Melbourne's Cremorne, a couple of suburbs over from the house's location in Armadale. The starting point for B.E Architecture's design was the site – an inner-city block where houses are set close to the boundaries and privacy is an issue. For this reason, the design was about creating an inward-looking house that is full of light but isn't exposed to the neighbours or to the street. The granite exterior was key to achieving this. 'Privacy is implied through a sense of solidity,' explains Broderick Ely from B.E Architecture. 'The stone element does enhance that feeling of protection, support and permanence.'

Three types of granite were used to wrap the exterior of the building, creating a permanent facade that doesn't need to be repainted or finished and won't break down. Rather than using a stone tile finish, the stone was cut in long pieces and laid by a stonemason, its distinctive split face creating a striking textural pattern. For the architecture team, stone was chosen not only to create privacy but also for its ability to evoke a sense of history. The granite was also brought into the interiors along the

∧ The open-plan living/dining space opens directly onto an exterior deck.

< The granite was cut in long pieces and laid by a stonemason.

∧ The kitchen's stainless-steel island bench has a dull finish that makes it look like pewter.

〉 An artwork of Ophelia in the lake by photographer Nadav Kander hangs in the living room.

≫ The living space is filled with art and objects, including Henry Wilson's Surface Sconce.

windowsills, while outside a 1400-millimetre-square block of granite projects out over the pool to create a small balcony. In the ensuite bathroom, a custom basin and freestanding bath were also engineered from solid blocks of stone.

Inside, the house has a muted palette, with grey materials throughout, including a concrete curving staircase, grey curtains, grey tiling and a sanded stainless-steel island bench in the kitchen that, because of its dull finish, looks almost like pewter. While still including guest bedrooms for the couple's visiting adult children, the house functions as a space created for the owners themselves. It has a shared study space, luxurious main bedroom and extra-large ensuite bathroom. As an added extra, the bathroom opens out to an outdoor moss garden on the first floor of the house, complete with three Japanese maple trees and an outdoor shower, which is used every day. 'The client says he only uses that,' explains Ely. 'He showers outside, rain or shine. He loves it.'

As well as designing the house, B.E Architecture also worked with the clients on their art collection, including framing some pieces they already owned by Brett Whiteley and buying new pieces for the house from artists such as Imants Tillers and Mark Hilton. The architecture was designed with the art in mind, with sculptures placed just so, and built-in shelves created for artworks to be propped on. A sand-cast bronze sconce by Henry

Inside, the house has a muted palette, with grey materials throughout, including a concrete curving staircase, grey curtains, grey tiling and a sanded stainless-steel island bench in the kitchen that, because of its dull finish, looks almost like pewter.

Wilson – a piece of artwork that also functions as a lamp – sits alongside wire sculptures by Peter D Cole in the living room. There is even a screen that shows video artwork – the moving images flicker like a candle and can be glimpsed from the hallway.

In the shared study, steel museum cases with glass tops allow precious objects to be displayed without getting dusty. Here, the owners showcase important items they have collected over the years, and family heirlooms, rotating them like museum pieces. On any given day, the case may show an objet d'art picked up during the owners' travels, or the passport, silver brush and tobacco case that were the only things the client's grandfather had in his possession when he came from Poland. By making objects like these prominent within the space, the architects place importance on the history of the family who lives here and the items connected to this history, creating a place that is intimately personal. In combination with the solidity of its exterior, there is a very real way in which this house serves as a fortress for happy memories.

⌃ A storage case has been designed for the owners' family heirlooms and precious objects.

⌐ Joinery conceals a drinks cabinet with metallic drawers.

‹ The curving stair in grey concrete has a bespoke handrail.

« Green creepers cover an outside wall.

∧ The bathroom basins and bench were engineered from solid stone.

› The bedside table has been built in.

» The bath is made from solid stone, in keeping with the all-grey theme.

︿ A solid piece of granite
extends over the pool to
create a small balcony.

ARMADALE HOUSE

LOCATION
Armadale, Victoria

———

DETAILS
House; 3 bedrooms,
4 bathrooms; 450 m²

———

ARCHITECT
B.E Architecture

———

BUILDER
LBA Builders

———

PHOTOGRAPHY
Derek Swalwell

Molten metal

The Surface Sconce is one of a series of sand-cast objects designed by Sydneysider Henry Wilson and made in a local foundry. Wilson started at the Australian National University, working on one-off furniture designs, before completing his masters at the Design Academy Eindhoven in the Netherlands. He thought that this would be his entree into the world of mass manufacturing, but instead the innovative Dutch school taught him a humanist approach to design that was about deconstructing the process and materials of design objects. From there, many graduates work on projects away from the spotlight of mass manufacturing.

After some initial success with the A-joint series of tables, Wilson started working with a local foundry whose opportunities were lagging due to manufacturing being taken offshore. The project started with an experiment in sand-casting metal objects and has continued. Dozens of objects are now available, from dishes to doorhandles and lighting, made in small batches and cast in bronze, aluminium and brass. Other items in leather and stone complete the series.

The Surface Sconce is simple in design – a domed cylindrical base fitted to a dish-like circular shade. The surface is pitted and textured to create a sense of history in a new object, and the material oxidises and darkens over time as well. 'Sand-casting is a pretty rudimentary process,' explains Wilson. 'Its most basic explanation is it's an impression in sand – you pour the liquid metal into the shape in the sand.' The resulting design is very bold, strong and weighty, while also having a patina that is immediately appealing, like an archaeological find from the Bronze Age.

SURFACE SCONCE

DESIGNER
Henry Wilson

——

MATERIALS
Bronze

——

DETAILS OF CONSTRUCTION/MAKING
Sand-cast bronze

——

PHOTOGRAPHY
Andy Lewis

Light Corridor House

+BCAA
chandelier

ARCHITECT
FIGR

—

DESIGNER
Christopher Boots

Ingenious restraint

Every square centimetre of this house in the Melbourne suburb of Richmond has been used to maximum efficiency, making the most of doing more with less, while also retaining a sense of identity particular to the owner/architect and his Eastern European heritage. Michael Artemenko from FIGR says the house was 'in a pretty bad state' when he and his family were deciding whether to renovate and extend or just move on. The roof was leaking, the structure was leaning to one side and the general impression it gave was dark and dank. On the other hand, the house did have some heritage details, such as pressed-metal ceilings and large skirting boards, which gave the interiors some charm.

Once the decision to renovate was made, Artemenko and the team at FIGR used this project as a test case to find ways to 'reduce the domestic container'. That is, they wanted to create a functional, comfortable, liveable house with as small a footprint as possible. The first step was to reduce the bedrooms by 400 millimetres, allowing a second bathroom to be built. The laundry was placed behind cupboards in the hallway and no walk-in robes were included in the design. 'We tried to keep things pretty compact. Just what you require – nothing more.'

The front part of the house retains its heritage features, while the corridor that leads to the new part of the house gives some clues about the transformation that has taken place at the back. A highlight window from the new part of the house allows

∧ Bedrooms were made smaller to make the most of the available space.

⌐ A second bathroom at the front of the house was created by reducing the size of the bedrooms.

‹ The timber-lined corridor runs from the front to the back of the house.

› The kitchen cabinets are made from Ukrainian birch.

light into the corridor, so when you are in the old part of the house, the new extension starts to beckon. On the threshold between the old and new, the last part of the corridor is wrapped in 4.5 metres of spotted gum. 'It's the link that ties the two together,' explains Artemenko. 'As you move through this space, it's quiet, almost like you're walking through a forest.'

The new part of the house at the back comprises a living room and a large kitchen with dining table. Here, FIGR made a conscious choice not to have one large, open-plan space as is common in many houses of the same size. It was part of their design intention to critically examine what is needed in a house of this size. By creating two separate living areas, the spaces are connected but can be closed off for different activities. Each of the rooms is clad in a different timber, with the kitchen featuring birch from the Ukraine – a subtle nod to Artemenko's heritage. In-between the two rooms is more storage, while in the kitchen the built-in seating doubles as storage and space for the air-conditioning unit. These make up for the lack of overhead kitchen cabinets, which break the sightline, are difficult to access and are a bit more expensive to install. In the living room, the tones are grey and brown, with a BCAA chandelier by Christopher Boots creating a focal point. The chandelier's angles complement and offset the sloping timber ceiling above, while the branching elements of the light in black and gold with white globes echo the neutral colour palette of the surrounding walls and details.

∧ The living room is intimate, but bright and open in contrast to the dark timber-lined corridor adjacent.

⌐ Mirror finishes and the absence of overhead cabinets create a sense of space in the kitchen.

< The dining space features built-in banquette seating that conceals the air conditioner and provides storage.

∧ A sliding slatted timber screen opens up the living space to light and views.

⌐ The side of the house was pulled in to create a covered outdoor deck.

› The kitchen and dining space can be closed off from the living room.

The connection of the house to the exteriors has also been carefully thought through. The redundancy of the side passage in terrace houses was solved by compressing the kitchen and dining area and pulling the line of the house in to create a covered outdoor area. This created a habitable verandah-like outdoor space that is connected to the kitchen. Because it is located on the side of the property and is completely covered, it is protected from the heat of the western sun and the neighbours cannot overlook. The window that faces the back garden has a sliding slatted timber door that can be open or shut depending on the time of day or year. There is also an option to open everything up to get a framed view of the back garden from the living room.

This house has been designed to create a journey from the heritage details of the old house at the front through to the contemporary, timber-clad rooms at the back. For Artemenko, this is a story – from dark to light, from old to new – with the added benefit of timber that links him to his ancestry, like a Ukrainian forest in the middle of Melbourne.

LIGHT CORRIDOR HOUSE

LOCATION
Richmond, Victoria

———

DETAILS
House; 3 bedrooms,
2 bathrooms; 110 m²

———

ARCHITECT
FIGR

———

BUILDER
Grundella Construction

———

PHOTOGRAPHY
Tom Blachford and Kate Ballis

Multifarious iterations

Melbourne designer Christopher Boots works from his studio
in Melbourne's Fitzroy, where each chandelier, pendant and lamp
is made by a team of artisans that includes musicians, artists and
designers. He works closely with his clients, more than half of
whom are overseas, to develop bespoke designs, with many of
his lighting designs offering a range of different configurations.
Boots describes his products as a palette of materials and a visual
language that clients can use as a starting point for discussion
of a bespoke work. 'Beautiful architecture will demand a response
that's not off the shelf,' he says.

The BCAA chandelier is a modular design made up of a
series of branching rods inspired by branched-chain amino acids,
the building blocks of life. For Boots, the natural world is an ongoing
source of inspiration and the forms of Euclidean geometry – the
triangle, the square and the circle – are the basics from which
everything comes. 'Bruno Munari said in the 1960s that these are
the base elements and you can play with them,' he explains. 'Design
doesn't need to be tarted up.' The BCAA is a modular design with
numerous variations, creating a sense of bespoke individuality
for each and every client – almost like haute couture.

BCAA CHANDELIER

DESIGNER
Christopher Boots

——

MATERIALS
Polished brass and borosilicate glass

——

PHOTOGRAPHY
Courtesy of Christopher Boots

West End Cottage

+ Archie armchair

ARCHITECT

Vokes and Peters

———

DESIGNER

Jardan

Cooking up a story

The architects of this house in Brisbane's West End based their design on the personal needs of a family with four small boys, while also adapting the classic Queenslander building type into a home for the 21st century. When architecture studio Vokes and Peters start talking with new clients about a brief, they ask for a 'narrative brief' – a practice that started when they designed a house for an author. By asking for a narrative from the owners, the design team learns more than they would from a standard architect's brief, which might list a schedule of rooms, some dimensions and a few images. Instead, they find out how the family lives, the things they value and how they spend their time. This allows the architects to emphasise the right places in the building.

The narrative brief developed for this house revolved around a love of cooking, with the kitchen firmly in the heart of the home, providing a social space for the family to congregate and share quality time together while meals are prepared. The family talked to the architects about the idea of a long family table in the kitchen, like the one the servants use downstairs in *Downton Abbey*, where one person is peeling potatoes while another reads the newspaper. It's a productive space, but also a social one.

The second requirement of the brief was that the house cater for four growing boys, who were given a wing of their own that leads directly onto the garden. The main part of the house (with its intact Queenslander-style front) leads out from the kitchen and

∧ The living room features built-in seating and shelving with classic Queensland finishes.

< A long table provides a space for family activities and interactions.

159

The kitchen has views out to the garden.

Overhead storage in the kitchen is made of painted timber and glass and incorporates a drying rack.

dining spaces to an outdoor space – the terrace – while the kids' wing juts out further into the garden and has its own exit directly onto the grass of the garden. This allows the boys to go down the stairs into the garden and race around the side of the house to the terrace and kitchen. Certain spaces were designed especially for the kids, like the oversized steps from the kitchen to the outdoor terrace where the boys can eat an orange or an iceblock without getting mess all through the house.

In the new part of the house, where the kids' bedrooms, bathroom and laundry are, an arched doorway in black lends a playful touch. This detail is 'inspired by my *Play School* days' says Aaron Peters from Vokes and Peters. A deeper than average windowsill in the kids' room is the perfect place to line up dinosaurs, and a little brick staircase to nowhere in the garden is just the right height for running up and jumping off. 'All of that just springs from the fact that the brief started by talking about the garden as being the kids' place,' says Peters. 'So we made it a little more playful than we otherwise might have.'

The house itself is in a flood zone. Due to council restrictions, the house has already been lifted above the previous ground level, but the architects lifted the front part 100 millimetres more to allow a garage at ground level. Stairs from the main living space lead down to the new part of the house, which is on a level with the outdoor terrace at 1 metre above ground. The foundations here,

The narrative brief developed for this house revolved around a love of cooking, with the kitchen firmly in the heart of the home, providing a social space for the family to congregate ...

as well as the outdoor terrace, are in brick – an unusual material for a Queenslander and one that was about connecting to the earth. The outdoor terrace breaks down a perceived disconnect between the garden and the house, while also bringing light into the home. A brick exterior wall with a built-in fireplace catches northern light over the top of the front building and reflects it back into the interior of the house.

The interiors feature white walls in the living spaces, white tiles in the bathroom and white marble in the kitchen, all of which create a subtle contrast to timber floors and furniture. Traditional bentwood chairs and newer pieces, such as the Archie armchair by Jardan, use timber to harmonise with the home's interior. The Archie armchair provides relaxed seating, its dark blue upholstery offering a subdued tie-in to the neutral colour palette.

Despite the brick and other new elements, the house does retain characteristics of a traditional Queenslander, such as vertical joint wood panelling inside, cross-brace motifs and exposed timber rails on some of the joinery, including the shelves in the living room and the kitchen cabinets. 'We have drawn over one hundred Queenslanders and are very well versed in the language and sensibilities of Queensland architecture,' says Peters. 'This project was about finding a language that is distinctly new and contemporary but is also sympathetic and celebratory of what existed before.'

∧ The outdoor terrace is built from bricks, an unusual material for a Queenslander, and has a built-in fire place.

⌐ The rear part of the kitchen looks like a hard-working scullery.

⟨ All-white interiors with timber floors lead to a bathroom with black mosaic tiles.

WEST END COTTAGE

LOCATION
West End, Queensland

————

DETAILS
House; 3 bedrooms, 2 bathrooms;
180 m²

————

ARCHITECT
Vokes and Peters

————

BUILDER
Robson Constructions

————

PHOTOGRAPHY
Christopher Frederick Jones

∧ The children's wing has a
black-clad exterior with a playful
arched doorway.

⌐ The back of the house sports
a distinctive brick chimney.

Affirmative charm

Jardan is an Australian furniture company that has been in operation since 1987 and under the ownership and direction of brothers Nick and Mike Garnham since 1997. When Nick and Mike started, they had eight staff and a small factory. They now have 130 staff and sell their work through stores in Melbourne, Brisbane and Sydney, as well as online. Jardan has a strong environmental agenda, was certified in 2014 by the National Carbon Offset Standard (NCOS) as a carbon-neutral company and believes in manufacturing locally and minimising waste. Jardan's original sofas, tables, chairs, beds, lighting, textiles and homewares are designed by its in-house design studio, the Jardan Lab. This is where the growing design team does its research and development, creating prototypes and moving products through to production.

Archie is an armchair and sofa series designed by Nick Garnham and Rod Carlson in 2010. Its exposed American oak frame is reminiscent of mid-century designs without being derivative. The design features distinctive paddle arms, joint details in the timber and a cross-stitch detail to the seat, which is firm thanks to its combination of foam and feather-and-down filling.

This armchair is emblematic of an Australian design success story. All of Jardan's designs are constructed in the Melbourne factory and they have an increasingly loyal fan base of designers and non-designers alike.

ARCHIE ARMCHAIR

DESIGNER
Jardan Lab

MATERIALS
Solid American oak frame, high-resilience foam seat with feather-and-down wrap and back cushion

MANUFACTURER
Jardan

PHOTOGRAPHY
Courtesy of Jardan

Noble Hughes House

+ Wing Contour armchair

ARCHITECT
David Boyle

—

DESIGNER
Grant Featherston

Rocking the fifties

With a cactus garden and a distinctly mid-century modern feel, this house, at first glance, looks less suburban Sydney and more Palm Springs. A passion for all things 1950s – including architecture, design, art and swing dancing – was the starting point for this house in North Balgowlah. The clients had the collectables and the costumes from the era and sought an architect who would be able to make the house to fit. That architect was David Boyle. 'They wanted to create a new house which drew upon some of that optimism of the fifties,' says Boyle. 'It's really interesting to have a connection to people who are really involved in the style of that era.'

As you approach from the street, this house has several unusual features. Firstly, the cactus garden that greets you at the front. Secondly, a garage door with a pastel-coloured geometric design like a piece of installation art. Thirdly, the house itself, which runs along the left side of the boundary, leaving the right side open so that visitors can enter near the front of the house or continue walking the full length of the building outside, through a Japanese pebble garden, a paved area with stepping stones and a pool and backyard lawn towards the rear. The centre section of this outdoor garden is covered by an upper-storey terrace, which provides shade, while a timber structure with decorative geometric patterns above creates a play of light and shade below.

Inside, the majority of the ground floor is made up of one large, long, rectangular block with sliding doors that open to

∧ Colourful cabinetry in the kitchen references 1950s design.

‹ One long joinery unit acts as the kitchen bench, a sideboard and built-in seating.

Throughout the interiors, the colour scheme creates a sense of character and stops the building feeling like an empty white box: a pink wall here, a red wall there, a green door here...

the garden at the side. The long living space has been divided using two large, central boxes that contain storage, hidden televisions and other equipment – they also serve as room dividers between the living room, kitchen/dining room and family room. Throughout the house, there are references to 1950s architecture and design. They can be seen in the built-in furniture that runs along the back wall of all three rooms, acting as seating, credenza and kitchen bench, then credenza and seating again.

The house has also been furnished with vintage pieces, which adds to its mid-century modern charm. The clients went to America to visit the Glass House (designed by Philip Johnson) and Fallingwater (designed by Frank Lloyd Wright), showing their passion for the style. To complete their vision of mid-century modern charm, they purchased other key pieces, including a number of vintage Grant Featherston chairs. An iconic Wing Contour armchair, in red, has pride of place in the main living area, while a rare B210 rocking chair is a highlight in the master bedroom.

Throughout the interiors, the colour scheme creates a sense of character and stops the building feeling like an empty white box: a pink wall here, a red wall there, a green door here, green flooring upstairs, red and blues in the doors on the kitchen island and a palette of similar colours on a series of vertical 'fins' that jut out from the first-floor exterior. From the street, these coloured fins create a sense of unity and character for the house. Boyle

∧ The family room at the back of the house features a pink wall.

< The light-filled hall has hard-wearing green floors.

《 A staircase leads from the entry hall to the bedrooms upstairs.

> The outdoor area is accessed from the side of the house via a deck that is covered by a geometric screen.

developed the colour palette based on muted colours and pastel colours from the 1950s. He also had input from the owners, who added a deep blue and a bright yellow to the mix – an addition he realised afterwards that it needed. 'A lot of that came from nostalgic references,' explains Boyle. 'That yellow was the colour of the living room of the house that the client grew up in.'

Playful, creative features abound in this house: the spiral stair from the bedroom terrace to the garden downstairs, the rooftop cactus garden that is viewed from the main bedroom upstairs, and the stonework added to the fireplace and a column that runs near the stairs, injecting natural material into a house full of coloured planes. But for Boyle, the most exciting thing about this house is how it has changed the behaviour of the family who lives there – two 1950s fans and their two teenage daughters. Moving from the old fibro house that was on this site to the new house has completely changed their relationship to the outdoors. They never used to go outside, but they are now avid gardeners, tending to the cactus plants and the Japanese garden, as well as the grass and vegetables out the back, and they spend a lot of time outdoors. 'It's very rewarding to see how this house has actually changed the way that they live and connect with nature and the outside,' says Boyle. 'It's been one of the most rewarding aspects of the house for me.'

⌃ The master bedroom has a built-in window seat and a rare Grant Featherston rocking chair.

⌐ The upstairs finishes are a mix of pastels with timber and stone.

‹ The ensuite has a subdued black-and-white colour palette.

> The garden runs down the side of the house, where a spiral stair leads to the upstairs balcony.

NOBLE HUGHES HOUSE

LOCATION
North Balgowlah, New South Wales

————

DETAILS
House; 3 bedrooms plus study, 3 bathrooms; 290 m²

————

ARCHITECT
David Boyle

————

BUILDER
Graybuilt Pty Ltd

————

PHOTOGRAPHY
Simon Whitbread Photography

Human design

WING CONTOUR ARMCHAIR

DESIGNER
Grant Featherston

———

MATERIALS
Plywood, foam, upholstery

———

MANUFACTURER
Grazia & Co

———

PHOTOGRAPHY
Courtesy of Grazia & Co

Designed in 1951, the Wing Contour armchair is one of a number of pieces within Grant Featherston's iconic Contour series. Grant Featherston was born in Geelong in 1922 and was a self-taught designer. After returning to Melbourne from service in WWII, he started work on the Contour series in 1951. Through the next decade, he gained celebrity status for his furniture designs, appearing on television to promote the ideal of modernism for all Australians. The Contour was the first of his designs, created before he met, married and set up a design studio with Mary Featherston.

Why is the Contour series so special? It was inspired by German and Scandinavian designs that lifted the chair off the ground using legs, rather than sitting on a solid block, but Featherston did not have access to the plywood moulding technology the Europeans were using. Instead, he experimented with bent plywood. The Contour chair features two sheets of bent ply that interlock to create the chair's iconic shape. Like its modernist counterparts overseas, the chair allows the body to lean back rather than being upright. The contour is designed to follow the shape of the human body, like a sculpture in relief. The wing version features a high back that cocoons the body in a person-shaped piece of furniture, like a hammock.

The Featherston chairs in the Noble Hughes House are originals. Grazia & Co is currently the sole distributor of authentic Grant Featherston pieces, which are made under licence by Gordon Mather Industries (GMI).

Doorzien House

+ Exhausted LED 1 light

ARCHITECT
Bijl Architecture

—

DESIGNER
Dean Phillips and Darkon

Line of sight

The design of this semi-detached house in the Sydney suburb of Kirribilli is informed by how the house – and the views of Sydney Harbour beyond it – is made visible as you move through a sequence of spaces. The architecture draws sightlines through the house and beyond, while also making the house permeable through glass apertures that punctuate the building. The owners of the house connected immediately with the architect, Melonie Bayl-Smith from Bijl Architecture, over their Dutch connection – the owners lived in the Netherlands for many years, and Bayl-Smith has Dutch and Lebanese heritage. For this reason, the house was called Doorzien, which means 'see-through' in Dutch.

When the project began, this house was like many other semi-detached houses: small, narrow and with a tendency for gloominess. But it also had something rare – sweeping harbour views out the back of the property over the treetops. Beyond a traditional layout – bedrooms at the front, living space at the back – a set of stairs led down to a small, dark bedroom, bathroom and laundry. Bayl-Smith and the architecture team at Bijl saw the potential of the downstairs space and excavated rock and dirt to extend the house downwards. One 3-metre slab of exposed sandstone bedrock was kept in the cellar at the back of the downstairs space, offering a reference to the land and the story of the house.

∧ The house boasts views of Sydney Harbour from both levels.

‹ Materials are transparent, like the white ceramic tapestry that spans two storeys.

⌃ The interiors are primarily white, timber, black and brick.

⌐ Built-in joinery provides shelves and storage for books and design objects.

〉 The design opens up corners to bring in light and create sightlines.

Light is brought in through skylights that run along the sloping corridor ceiling upstairs and bounce light into the walls without being direct or harsh in the summer. This light carries through to the lower level thanks to see-through glass flooring all along the corridor floor. 'Part of it was because we really wanted to connect the two levels, but it was for practical reasons as well, to bring light through,' explains Bayl-Smith. 'It's not just about the visual connection, it's about bringing real light into the house.'

The stairs were moved to the side of the house to give more space to the living rooms, both upstairs and down. The shape of the upstairs room was subtly altered and pushed out, to create a sense of expansiveness and also to encourage sightlines across the harbour rather than directly into the neighbours' backyards. In this sense, this house gains space by expanding like a balloon from its existing footprint into the dirt and rock below, and the surrounding space. The new design fills gaps to create an envelope that is subtly different, while providing a logical flow from one room to the next. This can also be seen in the main corridor, where the ceiling was lifted up, sloping to meet the existing party wall that is revealed above the old ceiling line as a rough brick wall without render. This brick wall gives character to the interior and creates a sense of space through a subtle shift in materials. 'It's good that the brick

The architecture draws sightlines through the house and beyond, while also making the house permeable through glass apertures that punctuate the building.

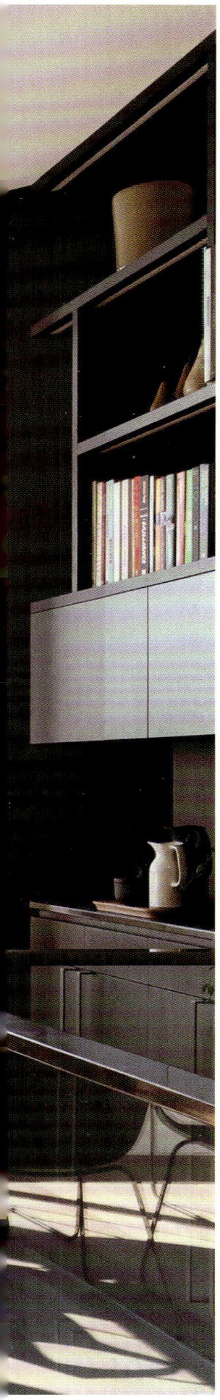

went all the way to the ridge. We did very little work up there and left some pretty dodgy brick action that someone had done at some stage. It's about the life of the house.'

Other design features of this house are similarly thought through in detail. Plumbing has been provided to the upstairs joinery space so that, if the owners are at some stage less mobile, they can connect a laundry to the top floor and live on one level, without having to carry laundry up and down the stairs. Likewise, the dressing room is designed with close attention to detail and for maximum convenience, with a central cupboard top creating space to lay out clothes or place jewellery. Every doorhandle has been designed specifically for the space. Downstairs, the world's first Redback solar battery has been installed and an inverter collects power from solar inserts in the roof that are camouflaged to blend in with the roof tiles. Stonework to the side of the house has been cut in large L-shaped pieces and laid to create a sense of solidity and quality to the building's exterior.

The joinery in the dressing room, kitchen and throughout the house has been beautifully finished, with a custom-designed downstairs desk creating a study space for two. Lighting is similarly simple but beautifully done, with Darkon providing strip lighting pendants in the kitchen, above the dining table and above the basin in the bathroom. Cylindrical tube lighting – the Exhausted LED 1, also by Darkon – is used in the wardrobe in a line of three lights,

∧ Black joinery continues in the kitchen, offset by the white and metallic island bench.

< The dining space in the living room is flooded with light and has spectacular views.

∧ The black joinery features bronze handles.

⌐ The wine cellar downstairs was dug from the house's foundations.

〉 A study space for two with a built-in desk has been created underneath the stairs.

while five cylinders have been clustered together into a chandelier in the bathroom above the bath. This simple collection of cylinders with small lights creates a sense of luxury for the bathroom, while also being functional and understated. An incredible ceramic wall installation, by local potter Natalie Rosin, combines with the architecture and design object and art selection to create a sense that this is a creative house whose views, though spectacular, are not its only asset.

∧ The door and window in the
master bedroom are framed
in black.

∨ The walk-in wardrobe includes
a bench for laying out clothes.

≫ Transparent floors in the corridor
allow light into the levels below.

> The exterior, clad in black
zinc, as seen from the rear
of the property.

DOORZIEN HOUSE

LOCATION
Kirribilli, New South Wales

———

DETAILS
House; 3 bedrooms,
2 bathrooms; 214 m²

———

ARCHITECT
Bijl Architecture

———

BUILDER
SKOPE Constructions

———

PHOTOGRAPHY
Katherine Lu

Pipe dream

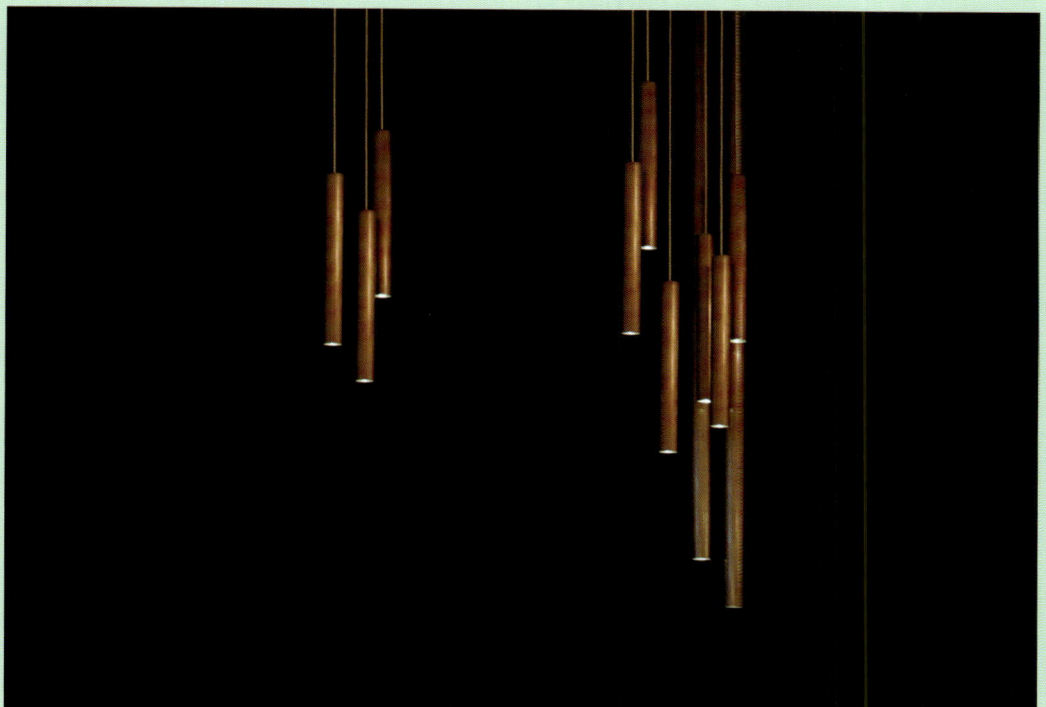

Dean Phillips was an industrial design student serving drinks in a bar when he secured his first leg-up in the design industry. 'They said, "Come work for us", and I thought it was the alcohol talking,' he admits. On the contrary, it was lighting guru Geoffrey Mance who offered Phillips his first job in lighting design. After working for Mance for many years, Phillips started out on his own with an eponymous range of decorative lighting, before starting his architectural lighting brand, Darkon. Now designing, making and selling both ranges, Phillips has a huge operation with several factories in Collingwood and a large staff. They focus on bespoke lighting, working with lighting designers and interior designers to come up with unique products based on the lights in their range or designed from scratch.

The Exhausted LED 1 lights in this project are clustered into a chandelier in the bathroom above the bath. These slim cylindrical tube lights are called 'exhausted' because they are made of exhaust pipe. Phillips originally designed them after he found a supplier that made a very thin steel-walled tube that wasn't overly heavy but was quite thin and delicate. He added a hockey puck–sized LED light to the base and the design was complete. A number of other related lights in different sizes were also supplied by the same company.

EXHAUSTED LED 1 LIGHT

DESIGNER
Dean Phillips

———

MATERIALS
Brass

———

DETAILS OF CONSTRUCTION/MAKING
Polished and chrome-plated exterior, linished brass interior

———

BRAND/MANUFACTURER
Darkon

———

PHOTOGRAPHY
Courtesy of Dean Phillips

Treetop House

+ Bronze table

ARCHITECT
Arent&Pyke

—

DESIGNER
Daniel Barbera

A curated vision

Combining two penthouses into one huge apartment across
a single floor gave Sydney interior design studio Arent&Pyke
a light-filled and expansive space as a blank canvas for the design
of this apartment. It was dubbed the Treetop House thanks to its
treetop views and large proportions. Sarah-Jane Pyke and Juliette
Arent had worked with the owners for years, getting to know
them and their style through the design of their previous heritage
home. With this new project, Arent&Pyke were brought on board
before the building was even constructed, which allowed the
design team to work closely with the base building architects
to ensure that the design would cater for the combination of the
two apartments into one.

  Having lived for so long in a period property, the owners
wanted to embrace a contemporary design that was clean and
crisp, but also had the sense of character that their heritage house
had in spades. Thanks to the spacious, light and airy quality
of the apartment, the designers replaced stark white walls with
subtle shades of pink and grey in the furnishings and tints
on the walls. The main open-plan kitchen and dining space
features huge floor-to-ceiling windows, with timber flooring,
grey marbled kitchen surfaces and a soft grey rug and pale pink
curtains adding texture and warmth. The living space is also
in pastel colours, with a beautiful pendant light cluster and
artworks offering points of interest.

∧ Each item in the apartment has
been carefully curated, including
this cluster of black-framed glass
coffee tables in the living room.

< Sheer pink curtains and a grey
rug soften the large dining space.

Having lived for so long in a period property, the owners wanted to embrace a contemporary design that was clean and crisp, but also had the sense of character that their heritage house had in spades.

The apartment was completely upgraded from its existing very basic finishes and fixtures, with new joinery, new floors, new lighting, new doors, new hardware and a new kitchen. The only spaces that didn't require a complete overhaul were the bathrooms, where tapware was upgraded and storage added. Some vintage pieces from the client's old house were reupholstered, but new furniture and lighting pieces were sourced by the interior design team, whose expertise in selecting just the right pieces is the result of decades of research. For Pyke, this means travelling to international fairs and places like the Paris Flea Market and keeping an eye on what's happening in design at both a national and global level. 'When you're a designer, design is your hobby,' she explains. 'You're constantly feeding your senses.'

Another key ingredient is getting to know the client, which the design team achieve through meetings, talking and, importantly, sharing imagery. Trust is an important factor, especially when clients say they want something different, and it is up to the design team to decipher what that might be. Arent&Pyke also advise on artwork selection, introducing clients to artists and galleries and borrowing works to see how they look in the space. This was not as necessary for this project – the client already had an incredible art collection, which the design team helped them to build on.

∧ The living space features furniture, artworks and rugs that complement each other perfectly.

< Living spaces in pale pink open to the balcony, which has views of the treetops.

> The kitchen blends white and grey marble finishes in an open and symmetrical layout.

Arent&Pyke also work closely with local designers, including Henry Wilson, who designed a custom brass handle that was used throughout the house, and Daniel Barbera, who created a hallway table version of his Bronze table. Rather than going with the existing proportions, the design team wanted a table that was higher than Barbera's Bronze coffee table and narrower than the dining table version. 'That's the beautiful thing about working with Australian designers – you do have that opportunity to get right into their practice. We have placed lots of [Barbera's] pieces over the years, but this is the first time we said, "Hey, what if we did something a bit different?" and he was really open to that.'

The process that Arent&Pyke undertake with their clients involves psychology – understanding the owners, their style, their taste and working with them to collect art and design – and curation – adding just the right pieces to assemble a new composition with a new aesthetic that meets requirements the clients didn't even know they had.

∧ Clutter-free spaces draw attention to the design and artworks.

⌐ The study has a timber desk and built-in shelves.

< The living room houses several artworks and a contemporary take on a glass chandelier.

∧ The bedroom has pink
curtains, a grey floor and
pale-green wall details.

⌐ The oak wardrobes are
lined in pink felt.

TREETOP HOUSE

LOCATION
Inner-western Sydney, New South Wales

——

DETAILS
Apartment; 2 bedrooms,
2 bathrooms; 260 m²

——

INTERIOR DESIGN
Arent&Pyke

——

BUILDER
Cumberland Building

——

PHOTOGRAPHY
Anson Smart

Liquid metal

BRONZE TABLE

DESIGNER
Daniel Barbera
———

MATERIALS
Bronze, marble
———

DETAILS OF CONSTRUCTION/MAKING
Sand-cast bronze, ground
and hand-polished
———

BRAND/MANUFACTURER
BARBERA
———

PHOTOGRAPHY
Courtesy of Daniel Barbera

Daniel Barbera is an industrial designer whose approach is influenced as much by his practical, hands-on father as it is by his industrial design training. Starting in 2004 with zero capital, he has slowly grown his business and now has a small manufacturing plant in Tottenham, Melbourne, making chairs, stools, shelving, tables, desks, mirrors, coat stands, lighting and outdoor furniture. The majority of the work is produced by a handful of staff working on his range of products in low- to medium-size volumes that are shipped around Australia and overseas. Almost all the materials are made or sourced in Australia.

Barbera works across a range of materials and each piece has its own story behind it – inspired by a particular brief for a commission, or self-initiated after an idea in the middle of the night. After first producing more commission-based work, the studio now produces a series of ranges, with custom work allowing designers to modify existing product lines.

Barbera's Bronze tables are made of bronze and Carrara marble, and inspired by the simplicity of combining these two ancient materials, used by the Romans and the Greeks since the time of early civilisations. Apart from a decision to design the table with three legs rather than four, the form of the table itself is, at least in part, determined by the nature of the material and the way that molten metal behaves in a cast. The resulting shapes are very organic, with gentle curves and a tapered leg. 'Liquid metal flows in a fluid way,' says Barbera. 'The beauty is in understanding what the metal wants to do.' The design is also logical and technically proficient – it is made with as little metal as possible. Barbera is preoccupied with working with the materials and producing classic work that will stand the test of time.

Kiah House

+ Black Sambuca
chandelier

ARCHITECT

Austin Maynard Architects

———

DESIGNER

Ruth Allen

House for a garden

A serene Japanese garden was the starting point of this project, designed by Austin Maynard Architects, in the Melbourne suburb of North Fitzroy. The owners had been living in the existing old weatherboard cottage with a 1980s extension, but the property had a poor layout with no connection to the beautiful garden, whose green plants pop up over and around a series of large and small stones.

The architectural response was, first of all, to cut off the old addition. Mark Austin likens it to a dashed line that you could simply run a pair of scissors across. The new addition consists of three elements: a master bedroom extending to the back boundary, a completely renovated kitchen in the old part of the house, and a suspended study on the first floor that provides a dedicated space for working from home, accessed via a spiral staircase. All three elements now look out onto the Japanese garden, which is the crux of the design. But it is the unconventional approach to the design that makes this project sing.

The master bedroom is designed as a contemplative space that connects to the garden. It is shielded from the back lane by black shutters that offer varying levels of privacy, including complete blackout. The bedroom looks out over the garden and is screened with a chain-link mesh that provides translucent screening to the exterior. The screens run on a steel frame made of black tubes that match the size and shape of the black shutters

∧ The spiral staircase and rear bedroom are accessible from the kitchen.

< The kitchen and upstairs study overlook the Japanese garden that is the centre of the home.

207

In the kitchen, the main design feature is the island bench, which has a sculptural feel. It is clad in timber with a stainless-steel section and a flip-up option that creates more bench space.

to the rear of the house. Sailcloths can also be attached to the mesh screens on hot days. In addition, the bedroom features a heavy curtain on a track that screens the bed entirely from light or can be tucked away into the cabinetry during the day. The shape of the bedroom is dictated by a huge eucalyptus tree, with a space designed specifically for meditating while looking at the tree. The bedroom also has a living green roof that can be viewed in its full glory from the study above.

The first-storey extension offers a solution for the owners, who wanted a space to work from home. This long, thin room has a study and shelves, with a window that overlooks the green roof and garden below, while the structure itself provides shading for the deck. This storey is accessed by a bright-red spiral staircase. 'We like using splashes of colour a lot in our projects,' explains Austin. 'We usually encourage owners to go for it and do something bold. It really enlivens that whole space.'

In the kitchen, the main design feature is the island bench, which has a sculptural feel. It is clad in timber with a stainless-steel section and a flip-up option that creates more bench space. The dining table is raised so that guests can perch at the table, while Ruth Allen's Black Sambuca chandelier ties into black elements elsewhere in the design.

∧ Mesh surrounds the top of the spiral staircase in the study.

⌐ The use of bold colour is a hallmark of the architects' work.

< The sculptural timber kitchen bench has a stainless-steel flip-up section.

The bathroom is dominated by yet another material – recycled red brick – with a sunken bath built completely in brick. If you want to take a shower, you simply cover the bath in a timber mat and stand on that. This creates a room full of texture and character. 'We wanted it to feel like it had been there in the past as opposed to the white or grey tiled bathroom with white plasterboard approach,' says Austin.

This project is not about selecting one material or one idea and going with it. Austin Maynard Architects are known for their unconventional choices and, in this instance, the client was all too happy to go with the red staircase, sunken brick bath and wire mesh on sliding rails. Most impressive of all is the mural on the first-storey timber addition. Austin Maynard Architects had worked with Seb Humphreys from Order 55 on another project, and when they suggested to the owners of this house that he might create a mural, they loved the idea. The resulting piece is subtle in its colours and, in photos, almost looks like a visual light projection. The idea of applying this directly onto the timber surface is not a conventional approach – that's the kind of detail that makes this project such a stand-out.

⟨ The bathroom features recycled red brick and a wooden cover that is placed over the bath to allow showering.

⌄ The sunken red-brick bath has views to a private garden.

《 The bedroom has views to the street that can be blocked by horizontal blinds.

‹ The bedroom opens directly
onto the garden.

› Curtains run on tracks around
the bedroom to block out light.

⌄ The bedroom's screens, blinds
and curtains ensure privacy.

∧ A mural painted directly
onto the wooden slats of
the first-storey addition
looks like a light projection.

KIAH HOUSE

LOCATION
North Fitzroy, Victoria

———

DETAILS
House; 3 bedrooms,
2 bathrooms; 163 m²

———

INTERIOR DESIGN
Austin Maynard Architects

———

BUILDER
CBD Contracting

———

PHOTOGRAPHY
Tess Kelly

Black bouquet

BLACK SAMBUCA CHANDELIER

DESIGNER
Ruth Allen

——

MATERIALS
Reclaimed manufactured Sambuca bottles

——

DETAILS OF CONSTRUCTION/MAKING
Reclaimed Sambuca bottles are washed,
cut and then heated and transformed using
traditional hot glass techniques

——

PHOTOGRAPHY
Liquid Photography

Ruth Allen is a glass artist who started working with recycled glass bottles in 2015, after other studies in sustainable materials. While the idea of recycling bottles into other objects isn't new, Allen took this approach one step further with the design of pendant lights – a process that took around nine months to perfect. She also experiments with different kinds of bottles, including champagne bottles, which are thicker and give her more to work with. The Black Sambuca chandelier takes its name from the tall, black glass Sambuca bottle, which Allen manipulates to create a tulip-like shape.

Allen has a factory behind her home in Melbourne and runs her business full time, working with at least one other person – a common practice among glass artists. 'Working on your own is not as joyous as when you're sharing the day with someone,' she explains. 'And you can produce a lot more.'

Allen believes that there are too many 'things' in the world and describes herself as a bit 'maniacal' about sustainability and conservation of materials. As well as using recycled glass, she also recycles all her water and has solar panels and water tanks.

Port Officer's House

+ XO chair

ARCHITECT
Birrelli art + design + architecture

—

DESIGNER
Rye Dunsmuir

Inhabiting history

A tiny block, just 4 metres wide, was the starting point for this house facing the water in Hobart's Salamanca Place. The last on the end of a row of 19th-century terraces that historically housed the crew who rowed their boats out to the tall ships, this is the original site of the Hobart Port Officer's residence from 1830, which was demolished long ago. Seeing potential in the small site, Jack Birrell from Launceston architecture studio Birrelli suggested that the existing remnant sandstone walls and the garage that had been built on the site could be redeveloped into a contemporary home. This solution not only created a harbourside location for his long-term clients but also raised funds for the retirement of the owners of the site, who also owned the house next door.

As the origins of the building go back to the earliest days of colonial Australia, the project had to undergo an extensive heritage and archaeological survey involving a large team of specialists. And since two-thirds of the building is underground, it was impossible at the beginning of the process to know what would be uncovered. 'It was more a mining exercise,' explains Birrell. 'We had a 10-tonne excavator on top of it with a concrete saw and all of this massive equipment.' Underground, they discovered an old cellar with wine bottles – 'Yes, there was wine in the bottles.'

⌃ Existing sandstone walls were retained downstairs, and skylights bring in light.

⌐ The main living space is simple in white and timber and has balcony views.

< The curving staircase features vertical timber battens.

∧ The master bedroom downstairs
has a freestanding bath and
timber joinery.

⌐ The bedroom has views to
the garden.

After several years of discovery, excavation, renovation and rebuilding, Birrell has created a contemporary home that also makes room for ample connections to its historic origins. The house is hidden from the street behind a narrow frontage with a front door beside a single garage door. The garage is decorated with a landscape mural by Birrell that depicts the Derwent River and Hunter Island prior to British settlement. It is based on historical photos and drawings from the time. 'I plotted where the island was and looked at historical photos and drawings,' says Birrell. 'One was a Haughton Forrest painting – you can see there's almost no development on the side of the colony.' To create the mural, Birrell's drawing was converted to vinyl and then silhouetted onto mirrors and corten steel.

As you enter the house through the door to the right of the mural, a corridor opens up to a large, open-plan kitchen, dining and living space, and the view out the back of the house is immediately apparent. Walking through the centre of the space, you are drawn to a balcony, which boasts a peaceful, inviting view of treetops, river, mountains and sky. In this open living space, simplicity reigns. The white kitchen, walls and ceiling are made inviting with the addition of timber window frames, balustrades and furniture, including a long dining table and a set of XO chairs in Tasmanian myrtle and leather by local designer/maker Rye Dunsmuir. Concrete floors create a contemporary feel. Skylights puncture the ceiling, bringing

in welcome light to the space, which continues down to the floor below via two voids on the left and right of the room – one a staircase leading to the lower floor and the other a double-height void framed in timber balustrades.

Downstairs, original sandstone blocks remain exposed in the main hall, bedroom and bathroom, creating a sense of history – these pick-marked blocks were almost certainly carved by convicts. In addition to these historical elements, the architecture makes the most of contemporary technology, using power from solar panels (the house is off the grid) and insulating materials, including double glazing and vapour-proof glass. The downstairs rooms open to the outside directly below the upstairs balcony. The house is a simple rectangle made with simple materials – concrete, timber, glass, sandstone. It has a rawness to it, while also providing a luxurious environment for living.

That this house exists at all is due to the vision of the architect, his connections with the community and the teamwork of the historians, archaeologists, heritage experts, builders, architects and designers who brought it to life. The result is a gem of a house – compact but functional and with one of the best views around. Tasmanian history is almost tangible in this part of Hobart and this house, from its contemporary mural at street level to its sandstone blocks in the basement, is a perfect embodiment of that history.

∨ A mural in corten steel depicts
the surrounding landscape as it
was before European settlement.

PORT OFFICER'S HOUSE

LOCATION
Hobart, Tasmania

———

DETAILS
House; 2 bedrooms,
2 bathrooms; 175 m²

———

ARCHITECT
Birrelli art+design+architecture

———

BUILDER
Cordwell Lane

———

PHOTOGRAPHY
Cherrie Eisemann, ACOMA

Timber
as skeleton

XO CHAIR

DESIGNER
Rye Dunsmuir

————

MATERIALS
Tasmanian myrtle (also made in oak
or blackwood) and leather

————

DETAILS OF CONSTRUCTION/MAKING
Traditional mortise and tenon joinery

————

PHOTOGRAPHY
Bruce Moyle

For Rye Dunsmuir, timber is a material that is not only beautiful but also gets better with age. Working in furniture and small product design, his practice shifted from working almost entirely with steel to working with timber when he moved to Tasmania to study at the Hobart School of Art, which was a major force in furniture design at the time. Now, his practice focuses on design and prototyping, and he works closely with local craftspeople to sell around a dozen products both locally and around Australia, while also working on one-off and bespoke pieces.

The XO chair takes its name from 'exoskeleton' – a skeleton on the outside of the body, which some insects and sealife have – because the timber structure of the chair extends past its leather seat. Dunsmuir originally created the chair and a matching table for a new cancer support centre. He took special care to get the ergonomics and access right – the low arms of the chair are designed to assist people with limited mobility, for example. The XO chairs in the Port Officer's House were an evolution of this original chair and are the only XO chairs made from myrtle, which was sourced through the owners of the house.

The Headland and The Range

+ Molloy table

ARCHITECT
Atelier Andy Carson

—

DESIGNER
Adam Goodrum

Rooms with a view

With an incredible 180-degree view onto rolling fields, rugged cliffs and sandy beaches, this site was always going to deliver on beautiful scenery. The owners of these two houses on a hill in Gerringong, 130 kilometres south of Sydney, had previously worked with architect Andy Carson on a completely different project – an adaptive re-use of a warehouse into a co-working space and design hub. This brief was for two contemporary homes for family and guests that offered respite from their busy inner-city lives. The main home, The Headland, and the guest house, The Range, were designed as contemporary dwellings that not only offer an amazing holiday experience but also recede into and complement the landscape.

The Headland is formulated around a U shape, with three separate but interconnected pavilions positioned around a pool, lawn and deck. The courtyard form of the house is a direct response to the windy conditions of the site. The lounge and living pavilion, and the bedroom and bathroom pavilion, form the majority of the house, snaking through the landscape, clad in black aluminium. The third pavilion, housing the garage, is timber-clad. All three pavilions are linked by external stairs and large glass doors.

∧ The Headland is made up of three interconnected pavilions.

⟨ The Headland's living room has views of the ocean.

⟩ Living room windows frame spectacular scenery.

∧ The Headland's kitchen features white joinery and a large black island bench with seating.

> The Headland's bathrooms are dark and cave-like, and protected from the elements.

While the courtyard typology offers protection from the wind, the orientation and shape of each pavilion is also dictated by the elements – twisting and bending to protect against harsh sun and wind – as well as making the most of the views. 'It's a little bit like a plant that grows towards the light or towards the water,' says Carson. 'The building, in its exact position, responds to sun and wind and views in different ways. If it was moved 100 metres away and we had the same approach, the form of the building would be completely different, even in responding to those exact same things.'

As you move through the house, each room offers incredible views across to the ocean, along the beach, over the property itself, and out to the Illawarra escarpment, which is 600 metres above sea level. In the main living space, a full-height glazed wall and balcony overlook Werri Beach. The house protrudes above the land in a cantilever supported by angled pillars, like an oversized picture-box window. Bedrooms and bathrooms feature oblique angles, each with a specific purpose and view. In each instance the view is framed purposely. The architect is acting not only as the designer of a building but also as the curator of stunning scenery.

As you move through the house, each room offers incredible views across to the ocean, along the beach, over the property itself, and out to the Illawarra escarpment, which is 600 metres above sea level.

The rooms are generous, with muted timber floors and rimless windows. They are, at times, sparsely furnished, with armchairs and matching footstools positioned serenely before large windows. The Molloy table, by Adam Goodrum, seats twelve people in front of a stunning view of the headland. Simple and unobtrusive, its touchable timber materiality adds warmth to the space. (A second Molloy table is featured in The Range – this version is a ten-seater and is situated between the kitchen and the living room, capturing views out to both decks and beyond.) The colour palette is neutral without overusing stark black or white, offering shades of tertiary colours combined with timber and metal, leather and upholstery. The house is environmentally sustainable and includes a 140,000-litre rainwater tank buried into the hill that collects water from the roof and has UV filtration and treatment for drinking. All sewage is treated on site and the house is powered by supplementary solar power. Both houses offer a passive design with extra thick, highly insulated walls and double glazing with thermally broken window frames.

⌃ A bedroom with grey interiors and caramel brown highlights.

⌐ A freestanding bath offers views of the escarpment.

‹ The bedroom features oblique angles and a window that frames a commanding scene.

The Range is a long rectangular building that features an asymmetrical roofline.

The exterior form of The Range mimics a classic farmhouse or shed.

The Range is set slightly away from the main house and is simpler, more like a rectilinear farm house or agricultural building. Its plan is inspired by the classic north–south oriented buildings by Pritzker Architecture Prize-winner Glenn Murcutt. Here, an asymmetrical roofline adds character and creates a vaulted ceiling, where the angles are clad in timber. Oversized manually operated lever blades at the end of the living space can be opened fully (to optimise the view), angled or closed, and create a striking design feature in copper. While the exterior of this house is necessarily more exposed to the wind, it features both a north and a south deck, offering different options depending on the season and the weather. The interiors provide a simplicity that matches the plan of the house, with timber cladding wrapping walls and ceiling, and concrete floors, furniture and rugs used to separate the large living space into zones.

The challenge for any owner or architect considering building on an undeveloped site is to create a building (or buildings, in this case) that is respectful of the landscape and makes the most of incredible views from the site, without ruining it for everyone else. Here, the sloping land and the escarpment allow the buildings to blend in with the landscape, while the choice of materials and dark colours recede the building as much as possible from view.

The Range is set slightly away from the
main house and is simpler, more like
a rectilinear farm house or agricultural
building … an asymmetrical roofline adds
character and creates a vaulted ceiling …

> A suspended fireplace and oversized copper louvres control temperature and light.

< The Molloy table by Adam Goodrum offers designer dining at The Range.

∨ A simple timber-clad bedroom at The Range opens directly onto the outdoor deck.

∧ The Range's living room has
timber-clad walls, teamed with
soft grey furnishings.

THE HEADLAND AND THE RANGE

LOCATION
Gerringong, New South Wales

————

DETAILS
House and guest house;
4 bedrooms, 4 bathrooms (The Headland);
2 bedrooms, 1 bathroom (The Range);
485 m² (The Headland); 125 m² (The Range)

————

ARCHITECT
Atelier Andy Carson

————

BUILDER
Bellevarde Constructions

————

PHOTOGRAPHY
Tom Blachford and Kate Ballis;
Michael Nicholson

Timber's grain

Adam Goodrum is one of Australia's most celebrated furniture and product designers, having come under the spotlight with his Stitch chair, which was manufactured by Italian brand Cappellini. For Goodrum, until recently, working as an Australian designer meant striving to get your work noticed by international furniture brands – a difficult task that meant facing global competition. All this has changed with brands like Cult, which first started working with Goodrum on a sofa. That single piece has now expanded into a whole range of furniture, including the Molloy table.

The brief was for a simple table – something that could go with different types of chairs. It had to be easy to ship – detachable legs solved this problem – but also be sophisticated and made with exceptional quality materials. The name, Molloy, comes from the island at the junction of the Blackwood and Scott rivers in Western Australia. As a reference to this, Goodrum wanted the grain of the wood to be visible, snaking like the rivers along the tabletop. 'With the Molloy table, I wanted to accentuate the grain,' says Goodrum. 'Its jigsaw component also shows the contrast of the different timber grains meeting in the one spot.' The Molloy table now has a Molloy chair, designed along similar lines, and the success of Cult's Australian range is starting to gain traction overseas.

MOLLOY TABLE

DESIGNER
Adam Goodrum

——

MATERIALS
Timber – walnut, ash or oak

——

DETAILS OF CONSTRUCTION/MAKING
Solid timber, legs made on a 5-axis CNC machine

——

MANUFACTURER/BRAND
Nau for Cult

——

PHOTOGRAPHY
Jason Busch

House A

+ Donny stool

ARCHITECT
Whispering Smith

—

DESIGNER
Guy Eddington

Rethinking
the plot

⌐ Built-in furniture in the living
  room is made with white tiles.

> Internal panelled walls are made
  from the same grey concrete as
  the kitchen benchtops.

House A is a project with a revolutionary purpose. Firstly, it is about using land intelligently, creating two houses – House A and House B (currently under construction) – on one block of land, as an example of urban infill, making the most of a large site. Secondly, it is about offering an alternative to the standard housing options in Perth, where project homes are dominant, design is undervalued and the houses are huge. 'There is not a terrific design culture here,' explains architect Kate Fitzgerald from Whispering Smith. 'The land is larger and the houses are larger. House A is anti that.' Thirdly, it is about presenting new design approaches to materiality and construction instead of conforming to a colorbond roof, gutter, brick and tile uniformity that has become ubiquitous in Western Australia (and many other parts of Australia), based on a false perception that brick means quality and the only other option is a badly insulated fibro shack.

Situated in Perth's Scarborough, House A has a timber frame with concrete panelling and, with a footprint of only 70 square metres, it is quite low-fi. There are no air-conditioning or automated light systems here. Any tech in the house is related to sustainable features, including an underground rain tank, solar panels and recycled materials. The layout is simple, with a living space downstairs, a long galley kitchen opening out onto a deck and a study at the back of the house, while a laundry and WC are tucked at the other end of the house. Upstairs, the bedroom

Inside, the approach to materials
and furnishings incorporates the kind
of built-in furniture championed in the
1950s by Bruce Rickard and Frank Lloyd
Wright, though with a completely
different material palette and aesthetic.

has a vaulted ceiling and is adjoined by an ensuite and walk-in wardrobe – simple, small and perfectly formed. Despite not having a huge yard, House A is connected to nature by the front garden, where native planting encourages birdlife and creates green space for the occupants and the neighbourhood. The soft grey of the concrete-panelled exterior complements the green landscape and reflects the pink of sunset – a complete contrast to the red-brick and tiled roofs of the surrounding suburb.

This house is very much a statement – an opening up of possibilities as part of a generational shift. Fitzgerald describes her studio as staunchly feminist, which gives a clue about the spirit of radical change that her architectural approach embodies. The house seems to shout, 'Things are different now!' All sorts of new materials have come on board – the construction industry should take note. 'There's a generation of people about to start building who are not looking at the houses in their neighbourhood, but are getting inspired by stays in Airbnbs all over the world,' says Fitzgerald.

⌐ Everything in the house is made locally, including the ceramics in the kitchen.

∧ The simple galley kitchen is all that is needed for contemporary living.

< The staircase is made of a single piece of wood, and has a brick base and a mesh balustrade.

> The view from the living room to the small walled courtyard out the back.

∧ The white frames and dark green velvet of the built-in furniture match the minimal interiors.

⌐ The grey concrete balustrade contrasts with white bricks upstairs.

› The built-in sofa in the living room is extended to become a tiled coffee table or bench.

Inside, the approach to materials and furnishings incorporates the kind of built-in furniture championed in the 1950s by Bruce Rickard and Frank Lloyd Wright, though with a completely different material palette and aesthetic. A custom-designed sofa features a white powder-coated frame and dark green velvet, and is connected to a low table of white tiles that is also built-in. The stairs feature a white brick base, timber main structure (crafted by a local joiner) and a white metal balustrade. For these, and other elements within the house, Fitzgerald called on friends and colleagues – a carpenter, a steelworker (even the concrete panels of the house were cast on site) – all part of a thriving design and construction scene that is growing in this part of Australia. Other furniture and design pieces were sourced from local designers, including Guy Eddington's industrial-style Donny bar stool in olive green, and the ceramics in the kitchen – 'down to every plate'.

With House B, the main house of this block, currently under construction, this is a local success story where the power of a rebellious frame of mind and a can-do spirit, combined with a global design sensibility, has revolutionised this pocket of Perth. Let's hope we see more of these innovative grassroots projects popping up around Australia.

⌃ The upstairs bedroom has a
   vaulted ceiling and is surrounded
   by a balustrade.

⟨ Concrete steps lead to a recessed
   entry clad in black timber.

The white brick bathroom has a simple white basin.

Rustic brass bathroom taps and greenery create a natural aesthetic.

The walk-in wardrobe upstairs features a low storage unit covered in white tiles.

HOUSE A

LOCATION
Scarborough, Western Australia

———

DETAILS
House; 1 bedroom,
1 bathroom; 70 m²

———

ARCHITECT
Whispering Smith

———

BUILDER
Talo Construction

———

PHOTOGRAPHY
Ben Hosking

∧ A contrast to the brick exteriors
ubiquitous in Perth, the concrete-
panelling of House A reflects
the light and colours of the
surrounding landscape.

⌐ Vertical black timber battens
line the concrete entry.

Industrial charm

Guy Eddington is a Perth-based industrial, product and furniture designer who also teaches at the University of Western Australia and is a technician in the School of Design's student workshop. He launched his business and online shop with the Donny stool a few years ago when he was working alongside a number of young designers at Midland Atelier, just outside Perth. Now his shop also features two tables and a desk, with other pieces currently in development. He is also working with a colleague on a separate venture, Edgar by Design, for which he developed a tiled outdoor table.

The Donny stool was designed to be utilitarian and versatile for residential and commercial settings. It was the perfect first choice for his online shop, as it is easy to produce in both stool and bar-stool sizes. With a simple construction, the stool is made of four pieces of laser-cut steel riveted together and powder-coated, with a timber seat screwed into the top. Its design references mid-century furniture – the tapered legs are a nod to French designer Jean Prouvé – and its aesthetic is industrial, with details of its construction celebrated rather than disguised. The olive green bar-stool version of Donny was selected by Fitzgerald for the kitchen of House A, along with a side table, creating an industrial chic addition to the minimalist interiors.

DONNY STOOL

DESIGNER
Guy Eddington

———

MATERIALS
Powder-coated steel, Victorian ash

———

DETAILS OF CONSTRUCTION/MAKING
Riveted laser-cut steel, timber seat

———

PHOTOGRAPHY
Natasha Duffield

Apartment 1906

+ Apollo 1906 table

ARCHITECT
Amber Road

—

DESIGNER
Yasmine Ghoniem,
made by Jonathan West

Fortune favours the brave

When interior designer Yasmine Ghoniem from Amber Road first met the owner of this apartment, he was wearing hot pink glasses, a band t-shirt and a pair of thongs (flip-flops). He had just come out of a divorce and was looking for a completely fresh start. The apartment in a high-rise in Sydney's Potts Point featured stunning views but had been stripped down to a concrete shell. The owner wanted a space that was good for entertaining and could allow him to have guests and house his art collection but that could also be easily shut up while he was away. Apart from this basic information, and his distinctive wardrobe, the owner was elusive about what he wanted. 'He didn't really give us a brief,' says Ghoniem. 'But he was up for anything.'

The final design is masterful in its functionality and unexpected in its aesthetic sensibility. The layout fans out from the entry, with a living room that flows around the corner into a dining room and then a kitchen space, and a master suite tucked behind the kitchen. The main living space can be transformed into a second bedroom through the use of a fold-out bed that is concealed behind a grey-stained panel. In the evening, a projector screen can be pulled down for screening movies, while by night, the bed folds down and a slatted timber partition screen creates privacy between this room and the dining space. A large laundry space was converted into a second bathroom, with a new European-style laundry tucked neatly into the hall. Built-in joinery was custom-designed throughout,

∧ A bank of black joinery divides the kitchen and the master bedroom behind.

⌐ Brave choices of material include the kitchen marble, called 'broccatello di spagna'.

< The kitchen features a raw concrete ceiling, black joinery and a rich red-and-gold marble splashback.

> The living space has chocolate-coloured timber ceilings and caramel curtains.

∧ A screen of timber battens creates privacy when the living room is transformed into a second bedroom.

⌐ At the entry, a terrazzo ledge sits beside vertical plumbing stacks.

⟩ The living room includes a fold-away bed hidden behind a grey panel.

making use of every centimetre in the 80-square-metre house. Even a spare 150 millimetres below a window in the kitchen was used for shoe storage, with textured pads for sitting on while you put on your shoes.

The materials and colours of this apartment are not what you would expect in a harbour-view Sydney apartment – no sandy neutrals here. Colours are muted and earthy and materials are varied, with unexpected choices, like the use of black timber joinery in the kitchen, teamed with a rich, deep red and gold marble called 'broccatello di spagna'. In the living room, it's chocolate-coloured timber for the ceiling, paired with heavy caramel curtains. The adjoining dining space features deep aquamarine blue walls with grey floor tiles and pink folding blinds. The dining space is dominated by the round black Apollo 1906 table with a faceted base, glass top and lazy Susan, designed by Ghoniem. A fabric-covered light with vintage ticking can be raised or lowered above the dining table. The kitchen was raised above the existing floor level to conceal services and there are new terrazzo tiles underfoot. The island bench was designed with a sculptural shape – a curved oval perched on two uneven columns. The larger column carries the services, and having two columns rather than a solid base means that the bench does not block easy access to the balcony.

Colours are muted and earthy and materials are varied, with unexpected choices, like the use of black timber joinery in the kitchen, teamed with a rich, deep red and gold marble … In the living room, it's chocolate-coloured timber for the ceiling, paired with heavy caramel curtains.

A bank of curved, black, built-in cabinetry divides the kitchen and master bedroom. It doubles as a ledge and robe in the master bedroom with a mesh front, and as storage for the kitchen. The bathroom is a work of art in terrazzo, with a custom-designed basin made of two intersecting planes with pink terrazzo forming the base (inspired by the owner's pink glasses on that first meeting). The large mirror above was custom-designed to house three ceramic vessels, handcrafted by the builder's mother, that hold toothbrushes and combs. Meanwhile, at the entryway, one last piece of terrazzo forms a ledge in front of a large column and beside three existing vertical plumbing stacks that were previously hidden behind built-in joinery. 'We realised quite quickly that it was from this vantage point that one could first appreciate glimpses to the harbour beyond,' says Ghoniem. 'So we decided to leave the three vertical service elements exposed and dress one in dark brown leather bootlace, wrapped from top to bottom and casually tied off at the hip.'

All the rule books say that, in small spaces, white and neutral colours are the best to make a space feel light and bright and open and airy. Ghoniem is not the kind of person who follows the rules, and the design of this apartment is all the better for it. Her detailed approach is powerful and ingenious, with brave decisions creating a space that is full of character, while also offering ample amenity and functionality.

∧ Both the bedroom and the bathroom beyond feature built-in joinery.

‹ The bedroom wall curves around the side of the bed.

The bathroom is a work of art with different shades of terrazzo and a custom mirror.

APARTMENT 1906

LOCATION
Potts Point, New South Wales

———

DETAILS
Apartment; 2 bedrooms,
2 bathrooms; 70 m²

———

ARCHITECT
Amber Road

———

BUILDER
Promena Projects

———

PHOTOGRAPHY
Felix Forest

APOLLO 1906 TABLE

DESIGNER
Yasmine Ghoniem,
made by Jonathan West

——

MATERIALS
Black-stained faceted timber base,
tinted glass top

——

DETAILS OF CONSTRUCTION/MAKING
1.8-m-wide glass top between a faceted
black timber base and rotating disc top

——

PHOTOGRAPHY
Felix Forest

Black as the night sky

This one-off table was designed by Yasmine Ghoniem and made by Sydney joiner Jonathan West. The table is round, making it flexible in the number of people who can gather around it (up to twelve). The centre of the table is faceted in black timber, and a single piece of round glass sandwiched between the base and a disc above creates a lazy Susan, a feature that Ghoniem says recalls 'that iconic Aussie trip to the Chinese for your weekly dinner'. A glass tabletop helps the table to recede visually in a compact space, while its circular shape allows for flexibility. If it was solid timber it would completely dominate the room.

The glass top also inspired the name 'Apollo'. The form is galaxy-like: black and see-through, evoking the sky at night. Ghoniem worked with West to create the table, as well as much of the joinery in the apartment. 'She gave me some initial sketches and we developed them from there,' says West. 'I really enjoy Yasmine's courage to be quite bold with colour palettes and finishes.'

ARCHITECTS AND INTERIOR DESIGNERS

AMBER ROAD
amberroaddesign.com.au

ANDREW BURGES ARCHITECTS
aba-architects.com.au

ARCHITECTS EAT
eatas.com.au

ARENT&PYKE
arentpyke.com

ATELIER ANDY CARSON
atelier-andycarson.com

AUSTIN MAYNARD ARCHITECTS
maynardarchitects.com

BAGNOLI ARCHITECTS
bagnoli.co

B.E ARCHITECTURE
bearchitecture.com

BIJL ARCHITECTURE
bijlarchitecture.com.au

BIRRELLI ART + DESIGN + ARCHITECTURE
birrelli.com.au

BLACK RABBIT ARCHITECTURE + INTERIORS
theblackrabbit.com.au

BVN ARCHITECTURE
bvn.com.au

DAVID BOYLE ARCHITECT
davidboylearchitect.com.au

DOHERTY DESIGN STUDIO
dohertydesignstudio.com.au

FIGR
figr.com.au

HA ARCHITECTURE, PRODUCT & ENVIRONMENT
h-a.com.au

LIGHT HOUSE ARCHITECTURE & SCIENCE
lighthouseteam.com.au

SMART DESIGN STUDIO
smartdesignstudio.com

STUDIO PRINEAS
studioprineas.com.au

VOKES AND PETERS
vokesandpeters.com

WHISPERING SMITH
whisperingsmith.com.au

FURNITURE AND LIGHTING DESIGNERS

ADAM GOODRUM
adamgoodrum.com

ARTHUR G
arthurg.com.au

CHRISTOPHER BOOTS
christopherboots.com

DANIEL BARBERA
barberadesign.com

DEAN PHILLIPS (DARKON)
darkon.com.au

ELLIOT BASTIANON
elliotbastianon.com

GRANT FEATHERSTON
featherston.com.au

GUY EDDINGTON
guyeddington.com.au

HENRY WILSON
henrywilson.com.au

JARDAN
jardan.com.au

JON GOULDER
jongoulder.com

JONATHAN WEST
jonathanwest.com.au

JOUNI JÄRVELÄ (POP PLUS)
popplus.com.au

KATE STOKES (COCO FLIP)
cocoflip.com.au

KHAI LIEW
khailiew.com

KOSKELA
koskela.com.au

NICK RENNIE
nickrennie.com

ROSS DIDIER
didier.com.au

RUTH ALLEN
ruthallen.com.au

RYE DUNSMUIR
ryedunsmuir.com.au

TRENT JANSEN
trentjansen.com

PROJECT PHOTOGRAPHERS

AARON CITTI
aaroncitti.com

ALEX REINDERS
alexreinders.com

ANSON SMART
ansonsmart.com

BEN HOSKING
benhosking.com.au

BEN WRIGLEY
benwrigley.com.au

CHERRIE EISEMANN (ACOMA)
acoma.com.au

CHRIS WARNES
chriswarnes.com.au

CHRISTOPHER FREDERICK JONES
cfjphoto.com.au

DEREK SWALWELL
derekswalwell.com

FELIX FOREST
felixforest.com

KATE BALLIS
kateballis.com

KATHERINE LU
katherinelu.com

MICHAEL NICHOLSON
micnic.com.au

PETER BENNETTS
peterbennetts.com

ROD VARGAS
rodrigovargas.com

ROWENA MOORE
rowenamoore.com.au

SIMON WHITBREAD PHOTOGRAPHY
simonwhitbread.com.au

TESS KELLY
tesskelly.net

TOM BLACHFORD
tomblachford.com

PRODUCT PHOTOGRAPHERS

ALBERT COMPER
albertcomper.com

ANDY LEWIS
andylewis.com.au

BO WONG
bowong.com.au

BRUCE MOYLE
brucemoyle.com

DAVID LINDESAY
davidlindesay.com

DION ROBESON
dionrobeson.com.au

FELIX FOREST
felixforest.com

GRANT HANCOCK
granthancock.com

HAYDN CATTACH
haydncattach.com

JASON BUSCH
jasonbusch.com

JONATHON NG (ITSUKA STUDIO)
itsuka-studio.com.au

LIQUID PHOTOGRAPHY
liquidphotography.com.au

MACARENA WHITTLE
instagram.com/mawhi.studio

MICHAEL KAI
michaelkai.net

NATASHA DUFFIELD
natashaduffield.com

ARTWORK CREDITS

ACKNOWLEDGEMENTS

I'd like to thank Paulina de Laveaux, Elise Hassett and the team at Thames & Hudson Australia for their fantastic work and excellent edits. I'd also like to thank Chris for his advice and for being a wonderful support, always.

∧ Peach and blue details in the living room of Kew Residence by Doherty Design Studio.

First published in Australia in 2020
by Thames & Hudson Australia Pty Ltd
11 Central Boulevard, Portside Business Park
Port Melbourne, Victoria 3207
ABN: 72 004 751 964

thamesandhudson.com.au

Design Lives Here © Thames & Hudson Australia 2020

Text © Penny Craswell 2020
Images © copyright remains with the individual
copyright holders

23 22 21 20   5 4 3 2

Thames & Hudson Australia wishes to acknowledge that
Aboriginal and Torres Strait Islander people are the first
storytellers of this nation and the traditional custodians
of the land on which we live and work. We acknowledge
their continuing culture and pay respect to Elders past,
present and future.

ISBN 978-1-760-76017-5

 A catalogue record for this
book is available from the
National Library of Australia

NATIONAL
LIBRARY
OF AUSTRALIA

Every effort has been made to trace accurate ownership
of copyrighted text and visual materials used in this book.
Errors or omissions will be corrected in subsequent editions,
provided notification is sent to the publisher.

Design: Claire Orrell
Editing: Lorna Hendry
Printed and bound in China by C&C Offset Printing Co., Ltd

MIX
Paper from
responsible sources
FSC® C008047

FSC® is dedicated to the promotion of responsible forest
management worldwide. This product is made of material
from well-managed FSC®-certified forests and other
controlled sources.